Ninth Edition

Sentence Skills
A Workbook for Writers

Ninth Edition

Sentence Skills
A Workbook for Writers

John Langan
Atlantic Cape Community College

Connect
Learn
Succeed™

The McGraw·Hill Companies

Connect
Learn
Succeed™

SENTENCE SKILLS: A WORKBOOK FOR WRITERS, NINTH EDITION

2 3 4 5 6 7 8 9 0 DOC/DOC 1 0 9 8 7 6 5 4 3 2 1

ISBN: 978-0-07-337169-6
MHID: 0-07-337169-6 (Student's Edition)
ISBN: 978-0-07-735374-2
MHID: 0-07-735374-9 (Instructor's Edition)

Vice President & Editor-in-Chief: *Michael Ryan*
Vice President EDP/Central Publishing Services:
   Kimberly Meriwether David
Publisher: *David Patterson*
Senior Sponsoring Editor: *John Kindler*
Executive Marketing Manager: *Pamela S. Cooper*
Editorial Coordinator: *Marley Magaziner*
Project Manager: *Robin A. Reed*
Design Coordinator: *Margarite Reynolds*

Lead Photo Editor: *Alexandra Ambrose*
Cover Images: *Laptop: © Tim Hawley/Getty Images;*
   Pencils: © Nicholas Monu/iStock; Phone: © iStock;
   Notebook: © Stockbyte/Getty Images
Buyer: *Laura Fuller*
Media Project Manager: *Sridevi Palani*
Compositor: *Aptara®, Inc.*
Typeface: *11/13 Times*
Printer: *R.R. Donnelley*

All credits appearing on page or at the end of the book are considered to be an extension of the copyright page.

Library of Congress Cataloging-in-Publication Data

Langan, John, 1942–
    Sentence skills : a workbook for writers: form A / John Langan.—9th ed.
      p. cm.
"Annotated Instructor's Edition."
Includes index.
ISBN-13: 978-0-07-735374-2 (Instructor's bk.: alk. paper)
ISBN-10: 0-07-735374-9 (Instructor's bk.: alk. paper)
ISBN-13: 978-0-07-337169-6 (Student's bk.: alk. paper)
ISBN-10: 0-07-337169-6 (Student's bk.: alk paper)
1. English language—Sentences—Problems, exercises, etc. 2. English language—Grammar—Problems, exercises, etc.   I. Title.
PE1441.L352 2010
808'.042076—dc22   2010004824

www.mhhe.com

Praise for *Sentence Skills*

"Clear grammar explanations are the greatest strength of this book. The explanations are easy for students to digest."
—Janice Heigis, Northern Virginia Community College

"Sentence Skills not only presents the concepts well, it offers ample engaging practice opportunities, creating the repetition necessary for student retention of those concepts."
—Michelle Abbott, Georgia Highlands College

"The exercises are plentiful and useful. I particularly like the way that each chapter provides exercises on each subtopic and then mixes subtopics together in a Review Test."
—Jessica Rabin, Anne Arundel Community College

"I can say without reservation that I am impressed with this text, and I would certainly recommend it to colleagues."
—Milton Bentley, Central Georgia Technical College

"The major strengths of this book are its readability, its accuracy, and its completeness. It may be the best of its type."
—Dennis Tettelbach, Georgia Perimeter College

"The book is well organized, concise, and comprehensive. Sentence Skills is not just for this one course. It is a great reference book. I encourage my students to keep it and refer back to it when any question about basic concepts in English arises."
—Stephanie Bechtel Gooding, University of Maryland, University College-Europe

"The Langan books truly provide the clearest explanations of grammar rules."
—Lisa Moreno, Los Angeles Trade Technical College

About the Author

John Langan has taught and authored books on writing and reading skills for over thirty years. Before teaching, he earned advanced degrees in writing at Rutgers University and in reading at Rowan University. John now lives with his wife, Judith Nadell, near Philadelphia. In addition to his wife and Philly sports teams, his passions include reading and turning nonreaders on to the pleasure and power of books. Through Townsend Press, his educational publishing company, he has developed the nonprofit "Townsend Library"—a collection of more than a hundred new and classic stories with wide appeal to readers of all ages.

Contents

x   Contents

PART 2 Sentence Skills 64

SECTION 1 Sentences 66

SECTION 2   Verbs, Pronouns, and Agreement   143

SECTION 3   Modifiers and Parallelism   231

PART 3   Reinforcement of the Skills   452

APPENDIXES   514

Key Features of the Book

Sentence Skills will help students learn to write effectively. It is an all-in-one text that includes a basic rhetoric and gives full attention to grammar, punctuation, mechanics, and usage.

The book contains eight distinctive features to aid instructors and their students:

1. **Coverage of basic writing skills is exceptionally thorough.**

   The book pays special attention to fragments, run-ons, verbs, and other areas where students have serious problems. At the same time, a glance at the table of contents shows that the book treats skills (such as dictionary use and spelling improvement) not found in most other texts. In addition, parts of the book are devoted to the basics of effective writing, to practice in editing and proofreading, and to achieving variety in sentences.

2. **The book has a clear and flexible format.**

   It is organized in three easy-to-use parts. Part One is a guide to the goals of effective writing followed by a series of activities to help students practice and master those goals. Part Two is a comprehensive treatment of the rules of grammar, mechanics, punctuation, and usage needed for clear writing. Part Three provides a series of combined mastery, editing, and proofreading tests to reinforce the sentence skills presented in Part Two.

   Because parts, sections, and chapters are self-contained, instructors can move easily from, for instance, a rhetorical principle in Part One to a grammar rule in Part Two to a combined mastery test in Part Three.

3. **Opening chapters deal with the writer's attitude, writing as a process, and the importance of specific details in writing.**

   In its opening pages, the book helps students recognize and deal with their attitude toward writing—an important part of learning to write well. In the pages that follow, students are encouraged to see writing as a multistage process that moves from prewriting to proofreading. Later, a series of activities helps students understand the nature of specific details and how to generate and use those details. As writing teachers well know, learning to write concretely is a key step for students to master in becoming effective writers.

4. **Practice activities are numerous.**

   Most skills are reinforced by practice activities, review tests, and mastery tests, as well as tests in the *Instructor's Manual.* For many of the skills in the book, there are over one hundred practice sentences.

5. **Practice materials are varied and lively.**

   In many basic writing texts, exercises are monotonous and dry, causing students to lose interest in the skills presented. In *Sentence Skills,* many exercises involve students in various ways. An inductive opening activity allows students to see what they already know about a given skill. Within chapters, students may be asked to underline answers, add words, generate their own sentences, or edit passages. And the lively and engaging practice materials in the book both maintain interest and help students appreciate the value of vigorous details in writing.

6. **Active learning strategies appear throughout.**

   Key chapters of the book feature *collaborative* and *reflective activities* which help make students active participants in their learning. Using group discussion, team writing, and student-generated examples, these activities lend energy to the classroom and strengthen students' mastery of essential writing skills.

7. **Terminology is kept to a minimum.**

   In general, rules are explained using words students already know. A clause is a *word group* having a subject and a verb; a coordinating conjunction is a *joining word;* a nonrestrictive element is an *interrupter.* At the same time, traditional grammatical terms are mentioned briefly for students who learned them somewhere in the past and are comfortable seeing them again.

8. **Self-teaching is encouraged.**

   Students may check their answers to the introductory activities and the practice activities in Part One by referring to the answers in Appendix F. In this way, they are given the responsibility for teaching themselves. At the same time, to ensure that the answer key is used as a learning tool only, answers are *not* given for the review tests in Part Two or for any of the reinforcement tests in Part Three. These answers appear in the *Annotated Instructor's Edition* and the *Instructor's Manual;* they can be copied and handed out to students at the discretion of the instructor.

9. **Diagnostic and achievement tests are provided.**

   These tests appear in Appendixes D and E of the book. Each test may be given in two parts, the second of which provides instructors with a particularly detailed picture of a student's skill level.

Changes to the Ninth Edition

Here are the major changes to this new edition of *Sentence Skills:*

- Writing assignments, review tests, and mastery tests have been thoroughly revised to further reinforce the skills and activities presented in the book.

- Most photographs now include writing prompts to promote critical thinking and get students writing about topics and issues relevant to their lives. In addition, the lively four-color design is bolstered by new part-opening and interior photographs that enhance the book's content and give today's visually oriented students even more help in making connections between thinking and writing.

- Dozens of contemporary items and references have been added to the examples and practice materials so that students see themselves in the pages of the book and can further relate to the material presented.

- The Online Learning Center, which includes instructional aids and resources for both students and instructors, has been thoroughly updated.

Helpful Learning Aids Accompany the Book

Supplements for Instructors

- An *Annotated Instructor's Edition* (ISBN 0-07-735374-9) consists of the student text complete with answers to all activities and tests. Throughout the text, marginal Teaching Tips and ESL Tips offer suggestions for various approaches, classroom activities, discussions, and assignments.

- An *Online Learning Center* (**www.mhhe.com/langan**) offers a host of instructional aids and additional resources for instructors, including a comprehensive Test Bank, an Instructor's Manual, PowerPoint Slides, and more.

Supplements for Students

- An *Online Learning Center* (**www.mhhe.com/langan**) offers a host of study aids and additional resources for students including diagnostic quizzes, a guide to electronic resources, plagiarism and the Internet, a study skills primer, learning styles assessment, and more.

Acknowledgments

Reviewers who have contributed to this edition through their helpful comments include

Janice Heiges, *Northern Virginia Community College*

Michelle Abbott, *Georgia Highlands College*

Jessica Rabin, *Anne Arundel Community College*

Kelly Dedmon, *Isothermal Community College*

I owe thanks as well for the support provided by John Kindler, Marley Magaziner, and Janice Wiggins-Clarke at McGraw-Hill. My gratitude also goes to Paul Langan, who has helped this book become even more student-friendly than it was before.

Joyce Stern, Assistant Professor at Nassau Community College, contributed the ESL Tips to the *Annotated Instructor's Edition* of *Sentence Skills*. Professor Stern is also Assistant to the Chair in the department of Reading and Basic Education. An educator for over thirty years, she holds an advanced degree in TESOL from Hunter College, as well as a New York State Teaching Certificate in TESOL. She is currently coordinating the design, implementation, and recruitment of learning communities for both ESL and developmental students at Nassau Community College and has been recognized by the college's Center for Students with Disabilities for her dedication to student learning.

Donna T. Matsumoto, Assistant Professor of English and the Writing Discipline Coordinator at Leeward Community College in Hawaii (Pearl City), wrote the Teaching Tips for the *Annotated Instructor's Edition* of *Sentence Skills*. Professor Matsumoto has taught writing, women's studies, and American studies for a number of years throughout the University of Hawaii system, at Hawaii Pacific University, and in community schools for adults. She received a 2005 WebCT Exemplary Course Project award for her online writing course and is the author of McGraw-Hill's *The Virtual Workbook,* an online workbook featuring interactive activities and exercises.

John Langan

Ninth Edition

Sentence Skills
A Workbook for Writers

1

Effective Writing

Introduction

Part One is a guide to the goals of effective writing and includes a series of activities to help you practice and master these goals. Begin with the introductory chapter, which makes clear the reasons for learning sentence skills. Then move on to Chapter 2, which presents all the essentials you need to know to become an effective writer. You will be introduced to the four goals of effective writing and will work through a series of activities designed to strengthen your understanding of these goals. Finally, walk through the steps of the writing process—from prewriting to proofreading—in Chapter 3. Examples and activities are provided to illustrate each step, and after completing the activities, you'll be ready to take on the paragraph writing assignments at the end of the chapter.

At the same time that you are writing papers, start working through the sentence skills in Parts Two and Three of the book. Practicing the sentence skills in the context of actual writing assignments is the surest way to master the rules of grammar, mechanics, punctuation, and usage.

Good writing skills are a vital part of almost every career today. The nurse in the above photo, for example, must be able to write clearly and effectively so that others understand the medical needs of her patients. What do you think could happen to a patient if what this nurse has written is difficult to understand because of poor writing skills? Now think about your ideal job and imagine how writing will affect your day-to-day responsibilities. On a separate piece of paper, make a list of ways that effective writing skills will help you on the job.

Learning Sentence Skills

Why Learn Sentence Skills?

Why should someone planning a career as a nurse have to learn sentence skills? Why should an accounting major have to pass a competency test in grammar as part of a college education? Why should a potential physical therapist or graphic artist or computer programmer have to spend hours on the rules of English? Perhaps you are asking questions like these after finding yourself in a class with this book. On the other hand, perhaps you *know* you need to strengthen your basic writing skills, even though you may be unclear about the specific ways the skills will be of use to you. Whatever your views, you should understand why sentence skills—all the rules that make up standard English—are so important.

Clear Communication

Standard English, or "language by the book," is needed to communicate your thoughts to others with a minimal amount of distortion and misinterpretation. Knowing the traditional rules of grammar, punctuation, and usage will help you write clear sentences when communicating with others. You may have heard of the party game in which one person whispers a message to the next person; the message is passed in this way down a line of several other people. By the time the last person in line is asked to give the message aloud, it is usually so garbled and inaccurate that it barely resembles the original. Written communication in some form of English other than standard English carries the same potential for disaster.

To see how important standard English is to written communication, examine the pairs of sentences in the box on the following pages and answer the questions in each case.

1. Which sentence indicates that there might be a plot against Ted?

    a. We should leave Ted. These fumes might be poisonous.

    b. We should leave, Ted. These fumes might be poisonous.

2. Which sentence encourages self-mutilation?

    a. Leave your paper and hand in the dissecting kit.

    b. Leave your paper, and hand in the dissecting kit.

3. Which sentence indicates that the writer has a weak grasp of geography?

    a. As a child, I lived in Lake Worth, which is close to Palm Beach and Alaska.

    b. As a child, I lived in Lake Worth, which is close to Palm Beach, and Alaska.

4. In which sentence does the dog warden seem dangerous?

    a. Foaming at the mouth, the dog warden picked up the stray.

    b. Foaming at the mouth, the stray was picked up by the dog warden.

5. Which announcer was probably fired from the job?

    a. Outside the Academy Awards theater, the announcer called the guests names as they arrived.

    b. Outside the Academy Awards theater, the announcer called the guests' names as they arrived.

6. Below are the opening lines of two students' exam essays. Which student seems likely to earn a higher grade?

    a. Defense mechanisms is the way people hides their inner feelings and deals with stress. There is several types that we use to be protecting our true feelings.

    b. Defense mechanisms are the methods people use to cope with stress. Using a defense mechanism allows a person to hide his or her real desires and goals.

7. The following lines are taken from two English papers. Which student seems likely to earn a higher grade?

    a. A big problem on this campus is apathy, students don't participate in college activities. Such as clubs, student government, and plays.

    b. The most pressing problem on campus is the disgraceful state of the student lounge area. The floor is dirty, the chairs are torn, and the ceiling leaks.

continued

8. The following sentences are taken from reports by two employees. Which worker is more likely to be promoted?

    a. The spring line failed by 20 percent in the meeting of projected profit expectations. Which were issued in January of this year.

    b. Profits from our spring line were disappointing. They fell 20 percent short of January's predictions.

9. The following paragraphs are taken from two job application letters. Which applicant would you favor?

    a. Let me say in closing that their are an array of personal qualities I have presented in this letter, together, these make me hopeful of being interviewed for this attraktive position.
    sincerely yours'
    Brian Davis

    b. I feel I have the qualifications needed to do an excellent job as assistant manager of the jewelry department at Horton's. I look forward to discussing the position further at a personal interview.
    Sincerely yours,
    Richard O'Keeney

In each case, the first choice (*a*) contains sentence-skills mistakes. These mistakes include missing or misplaced commas and misspellings. As a result of such mistakes, clear communication cannot occur—and misunderstandings, lower grades, and missed job opportunities are probable results. The point, then, is that all the rules that make up standard written English should be a priority if you want your writing to be clear and effective.

Success in College

Standard English is essential if you want to succeed in college. Any report, paper, review, essay exam, or assignment you are responsible for should be written in the best standard English you can produce. If you don't do this, it won't matter how fine your ideas are or how hard you worked—most likely, you will receive a lower grade than you would otherwise deserve. In addition, because standard English requires you to express your thoughts in precise, clear sentences, training yourself to follow the rules can help you think more logically. The basic logic you learn to practice at the sentence level will help as you work to produce well-reasoned papers in all your subjects.

Success at Work

Knowing standard English will also help you achieve success on the job. Studies have found repeatedly that skillful communication, more than any other factor, is the key to job satisfaction and steady progress in a career. A solid understanding of standard English is a basic part of this vital ability to communicate. Moreover, most experts agree that we are now living in an "age of information"—a time when people who use language skillfully have a great advantage over those who do not. Fewer of us will be working in factories or at other types of manual labor. Many more of us will be working with information in various forms—accumulating it, processing it, analyzing it. No matter what kind of job you are preparing yourself for, technical or not, you will need to know standard English to keep pace with this new age. Otherwise, you are likely to be left behind, limited to low-paying jobs that offer few challenges or financial rewards.

"Oh, good heavens. We already know EVERYTHING about you. The resume is just to see if you can write a complete sentence." The above cartoon takes a humorous look at the importance of a clearly written resume. What does a poorly written resume say about a job applicant? Why is it important to have a clearly written, understandable resume? On a separate sheet of paper, list five ways a clearly written resume can help you in a job interview.

www.mhhe.com/langan

Success in Everyday Life

Standard English will help you succeed not just at school and work but in everyday life as well. It will help you feel more comfortable, for example, in writing letters to friends and relatives. It will enable you to write effective notes to your children's schools. It will help you get action when you write a letter of complaint to a company about a product. It will allow you to write letters inquiring about bills—hospital, medical, utility, or legal—or about any kind of service. To put it simply, in our daily lives, those who can use and write standard English have more power than those who cannot.

Your Attitude about Writing

Your attitude toward writing is an important part of learning to write well. To get a sense of just how you feel about writing, read the following statements. Put a check beside those statements with which you agree. (This activity is not a test, so try to be as honest as possible.)

_____ 1. A good writer should be able to sit down and write a paper straight through without stopping.

_____ 2. Writing is a skill that anyone can learn with practice.

_____ 3. I'll never be good at writing, because I make too many mistakes in spelling, grammar, and punctuation.

_____ 4. Because I dislike writing, I always start a paper at the last possible minute.

_____ 5. I've always done poorly in English, and I don't expect that to change.

Now read the following comments about these five statements. The comments will help you see if your attitude is hurting or helping your efforts to become a better writer.

1. **A good writer should be able to sit down and write a paper straight through without stopping.**

   The statement is *false*. Writing is, in fact, a process. It is done not in one easy step but in a series of steps, and seldom at one sitting. If you cannot do a paper all at once, you are like most of the other people on the planet. It is harmful to carry around the false idea that writing should be easy.

2. **Writing is a skill that anyone can learn with practice.**

   This statement is *absolutely true*. Writing is a skill, like driving or cooking, that you can master with hard work. If you want to learn to write, you can. It is as simple as that. If you believe this, you are ready to learn how to become a competent writer.

   Some people hold the false belief that writing is a natural gift, which some have and others do not. Because of this belief, they never make a truly honest effort to learn to write—and so they never learn.

3. **I'll never be good at writing, because I make too many mistakes in spelling, grammar, and punctuation.**

   The first concern in good writing should be *content*—what you have to say. Your ideas and feelings are what matter most. You should not worry about spelling, grammar, and punctuation while working on content.

   Unfortunately, some people are so self-conscious about making mistakes that they do not focus on what they want to say. They need to realize that a paper is best done in stages and that the rules can and should wait until a later stage in the writing process. Through review and practice, you will eventually learn how to follow the rules with confidence.

4. **Because I dislike writing, I always start a paper at the last minute.**

   This practice is all too common. You feel you are *going to* do poorly, and then your behavior ensures that you *will* do poorly! Your attitude is so negative that you defeat yourself—not even allowing enough time to really try.

   Again, what you need to realize is that writing is a process. Because it is done in steps, you don't have to get it right all at once. Just get started well in advance. If you allow yourself enough time, you'll find a way to make a paper come together.

5. **I've done poorly in English in the past, and I don't expect that to change now.**

   How you may have performed in the *past* does not control how you can perform in the *present*. Even if you did poorly in English in high school, it is in your power to make this one of your best subjects in college. If you believe writing can be learned, and if you work hard at it, you *will* become a better writer.

In brief, your attitude is crucial. If you believe you are a poor writer and always will be, chances are you will not improve. If you realize you can become a better writer, chances are you will improve. Depending on how you allow yourself to think, you can be your own best friend or your own worst enemy.

How This Book Is Organized

- A good way to get a quick sense of any book is to turn to the table of contents. By referring to the Contents pages, you will see that the book is organized into three basic parts. What are they?

  Part One: Effective Writing

  Part Two: Sentence Skills

  Part Three: Reinforcement of the Skills

- In Part One, the final section of Chapter 3 includes assignments in the *writing process*.

- Part Two deals with sentence skills. The first section is "Sentences." How many sections (skills areas) are covered in all? Count them. *five*

- Part Three reinforces the skills presented in Part Two. What are the three kinds of reinforcement activities in Part Three?

  Combined Mastery Tests

  Editing and Proofreading Tests

  Combined Editing Tests

- Finally, the six appendixes at the end of the book are: *(A) How a Computer Can Help, (B) Parts of Speech, (C) ESL Pointers, (D) Sentence-Skills Diagnostic Test, (E) Sentence-Skills Achievement Test, (F) Answers to Introductory Activities and Practice Exercises in Part Two.*

How to Use This Book

Here is a way to use *Sentence Skills*. First, read and work through Part One, Effective Writing—a guide to the goals of effective writing followed by a series of activities to help you practice and master these goals. Your instructor may direct you to certain activities, depending on your needs.

Second, take the diagnostic test on pages 546–551. By analyzing which sections of the test give you trouble, you will discover which skills you need to concentrate on. When you turn to an individual skill in Part Two, begin by reading and thinking about the introductory activity. Often you will be pleasantly surprised to find that you know more about this area of English than you thought you did. After all, you have probably been speaking English with fluency and ease for many years; you have an instinctive knowledge of how the language works. This knowledge gives you a solid base for refining your skills.

Your third step is to work on the skills in Part Two by reading the explanations and completing the practices. You can check your answers to each practice activity in this part by turning to the answer key at the back of the book (Appendix F). For any answers you got wrong, try to figure out *why* you got them wrong—you want to uncover any weak spots in your understanding.

Your next step is to use the review tests and mastery tests at the end of each chapter in Part Two to evaluate your understanding of a skill in its entirety. Your instructor may also ask you to take the other reinforcement tests in Part Three of the book. To help ensure that you take the time needed to learn each skill thoroughly, the answers to these tests are *not* in the answer key.

The emphasis in this book is on writing clear, error-free sentences. And the heart of the book is the practice material that helps reinforce the sentence skills you learn. A great deal of effort has been taken to make the practices lively and engaging and to avoid the dull, repetitive skills work that has given grammar books such a bad reputation. This text will help you stay interested as you work on the rules of English that you need to learn. The rest is a matter of your personal determination and hard work. If you decide—and only you can decide—that effective writing is important to your school and career goals and that you want to learn the basic skills needed to write clearly and effectively, this book will help you reach those goals.

A Brief Guide to Effective Writing

2

This chapter and Chapter 3 will show you how to write effective paragraphs. The following questions will be answered in turn:

1. What is a paragraph?
2. What are the goals of effective writing?
3. How do you reach the goals of effective writing?

What Is a Paragraph?

A *paragraph* is a series of sentences about one main idea, or *point*. A paragraph typically starts with a point, and the rest of the paragraph provides specific details to support and develop that point.

Consider the following paragraph, written by a student named Gary Callahan.

www.mhhe.com/langan

Returning to School

Starting college at age twenty-nine was difficult. For one thing, I did not have much support from my parents and friends. My father asked, "Didn't you get dumped on enough in high school? Why go back for more?" My mother worried about where the money would come from. My friends seemed threatened. "Hey, there's the college man," they would say when they saw me. Another reason that starting college was hard was that I had bad memories of school. I had spent years of my life sitting in classrooms

continued

> completely bored, watching clocks tick ever so slowly toward the final bell. When I was not bored, I was afraid of being embarrassed. Once a teacher called on me and then said, "Ah, forget it, Callahan," when he realized I did not know the answer. Finally, I soon learned that college would give me little time with my family. After work every day, I have just an hour and ten minutes to eat and spend time with my wife and daughter before going off to class. When I get back, my daughter is in bed, and my wife and I have only a little time together. Then the weekends go by quickly, with all the home-work I have to do. But I am going to persist because I believe a better life awaits me with a college degree.

The preceding paragraph, like many effective paragraphs, starts by stating a main idea, or point. A *point* is a general idea that contains an opinion. In this case, the point is that starting college at age twenty-nine was not easy.

In our everyday lives, we constantly make points about all kinds of matters. We express all kinds of opinions: "It's fun to connect with old friends on Facebook." "That was a terrible movie." "My psychology instructor is the best teacher I have ever had." "Eating at that restaurant was a mistake." "That team should win the playoff game." "Waitressing is the worst job I ever had." "Our state should allow the death penalty." "Cigarette smoking should be banned everywhere." "I prefer to read newspapers online instead of picking one up at the 7-11." In *talking* to people, we don't always give the reasons for our opinions. But in *writing,* we *must* provide reasons to support our ideas. Only by supplying solid evidence for any point that we make can we communicate effectively with readers.

An effective paragraph, then, must not only make a point but support it with *specific evidence*—reasons, examples, and other details. Such specifics help prove to readers that the point is reasonable. Even if readers do not agree with the writer, at least they have in front of them the evidence on which the writer has based his or her opinion. Readers are like juries; they want to see the evidence so that they can make their own judgments.

Take a moment now to examine the evidence that Gary has provided to back up his point about starting college at twenty-nine. Complete the following outline of Gary's paragraph by summarizing in a few words his reasons and the details that develop them. The first reason and its supporting details are summarized for you as an example.

POINT: Starting college at age twenty-nine was difficult.

REASON 1: *Little support from parents and friends*

DETAILS THAT DEVELOP REASON 1: *Father asked why I wanted to be*
dumped on again, mother worried about tuition money, friends seemed
threatened

REASON 2: _____

DETAILS THAT DEVELOP REASON 2: _____

REASON 3: _____

DETAILS THAT DEVELOP REASON 3: _____

_____

_____

As the outline makes clear, Gary provides three reasons to support his point about starting college at twenty-nine: (1) he had little support from his friends or parents, (2) he had bad memories of school, and (3) college left him little time with his family. Gary also provides vivid details to back up each of his three reasons. His reasons and descriptive details enable readers to see why he feels that starting college at twenty-nine was difficult.

To write an effective paragraph, then, aim to do what Gary has done: begin by making a point, and then go on to support that point with specific evidence. Finally, like Gary, end your paper with a sentence that rounds off the paragraph and provides a sense of completion.

Why are you in college? On a separate piece of paper, write a sentence on why you are in college and then list three reasons that support your main point for being in college.

The Goals of Effective Writing

Now that you have considered an effective student paragraph, it is time to look at four goals of effective writing.

Goal 1: Make a Point

It is often best to state your point in the first sentence of your paper, just as Gary does in his paragraph about returning to school. The sentence that expresses the main idea, or point, of a paragraph is called the *topic sentence.* Your paper will be unified if you make sure that all the details support the point in your topic sentence. Activities on pages 15–18 will help you learn how to write a topic sentence.

Goal 2: Support the Point

To support your point, you need to provide specific reasons, examples, and other details that explain and develop it. The more precise and particular your supporting details are, the better your readers can "see," "hear," and "feel" them. Activities on pages 18–33 will help you learn how to be specific in your writing.

Goal 3: Organize the Support

You will find it helpful to learn two common ways of organizing support in a paragraph—*listing order* and *time order.* You should also learn the signal words, known as *transitions,* that increase the effectiveness of each method. Activities on pages 33–40 will give you practice in the use of listing order and time order, as well as transitions, to organize the supporting details of a paragraph.

Goal 4: Write Error-Free Sentences

If you use correct spelling and follow the rules of grammar, punctuation, and usage, your sentences will be clear and well written. But by no means must you have all that information in your head. Even the best of writers need to use reference materials to be sure their writing is correct. So when you write your papers, keep a good dictionary and grammar handbook (you can use Part Two of this book) nearby.

In general, however, save them for after you've gotten your ideas firmly down in writing. You'll see in the next part of this guide that Gary made a number of sentence errors as he worked on his paragraph. But he simply ignored them until he got to a later draft of his paper, when there would be time enough to make the needed corrections.

Activities in the Goals of Effective Writing

The following series of activities will strengthen your understanding of the four goals of effective writing and how to reach those goals. The practice will also help you prepare for the demands of your college classes.

Your instructor may ask you to do the entire series of activities or may select those activities most suited to your particular needs.

www.mhhe.com/langan

Activities in Goal 1: Make a Point

Effective writing advances a point, or main idea, in a general statement known as the *topic sentence*. Other sentences in the paragraph provide specific support for the topic sentence.

The activities in this section will give you practice in the following:

> • Identifying the Point
> • Understanding the Topic Sentence
> • Identifying Topics, Topic Sentences, and Support

Identifying the Point

Each group of sentences below could be written as a short paragraph. Circle the letter of the topic sentence in each case. To find the topic sentence, ask yourself, "Which is a general statement supported by the specific details in the other three statements?"

Begin by trying the example below. First circle the letter of the sentence you think expresses the main idea. Then read the explanation.

Activity

1

EXAMPLE

    a. Newspapers are a good source of local, national, and world news.

    b. The cartoons and crossword puzzles in newspapers are entertaining.

    (c.) Newspapers have a lot to offer.

    d. Newspapers often include coupons worth far more than the cost of the paper.

> **EXPLANATION**   Sentence *a* explains one important benefit of newspapers. Sentences *b* and *d* provide other specific advantages of newspapers. In sentence *c*, however, no one specific benefit is explained. Instead, the words "a lot to offer" refer only generally to such benefits. Therefore sentence *c* is the topic sentence; it expresses the main idea. The other sentences support that idea by providing examples.

1. a. Even when Food City is crowded, there are only two cash registers open.
    b. The frozen foods are often partially thawed.
    c. I will never shop at Food City again.
    d. The market doesn't accept Internet coupons.

2. a. Buy only clothes that will match what's already in your closet.
    b. To be sure you're getting the best price, shop in a number of stores before buying.
    c. Avoid trendy clothes; buy basic pieces that never go out of style.
    d. By following a few simple rules, you can have nice clothes without spending a fortune.

3. a. Once my son said a vase jumped off the shelf by itself.
    b. When my son breaks something, he always has an excuse.
    c. He claimed that my three-month-old daughter climbed out of her crib and knocked a glass over.
    d. Another time, he said an earthquake must have caused a mirror to crack.

4. a. Mars should be the first planet explored by astronauts.
    b. Astronauts could mine Mars for aluminum, magnesium, and iron.
    c. The huge volcano on Mars would be fascinating to study.
    d. Since Mars is close to Earth, we might want to have colonies there one day.

5. a. Instead of talking on the telephone, we send text-messages.
    b. People rarely talk to one another these days.
    c. Rather than talking with family members, we sit silently in front of our TV sets all evening.
    d. In cars, we ignore our traveling companions to listen to the radio.

Understanding the Topic Sentence

As already explained, most paragraphs center on a main idea, which is often expressed in a topic sentence. An effective topic sentence does two things. First, it presents the topic of the paragraph. Second, it expresses the writer's attitude or opinion or idea about the topic. For example, look at the following topic sentence:

> Professional athletes are overpaid.

In the topic sentence, the topic is *professional athletes;* the writer's idea about the topic is that professional athletes *are overpaid.*

For each topic sentence below, underline the topic and double-underline the point of view that the writer takes toward the topic.

Activity

2

EXAMPLES

Living in a small town has many advantages.

Talking on a cell phone while driving should be banned in every state.

1. The apartments on Walnut Avenue are a fire hazard.

2. Losing my job turned out to have benefits.

3. Blues is the most interesting form of American music.

4. Our neighbor's backyard is a dangerous place.

5. Paula and Jeff are a stingy couple.

6. Snakes do not deserve their bad reputation.

7. Pollution causes many problems in American cities.

8. New fathers should receive "paternity leave."

9. People with low self-esteem often need to criticize others.

10. Learning to write effectively is largely a matter of practice.

Identifying Topics, Topic Sentences, and Support

The following activity will sharpen your sense of the differences between topics, topic sentences, and supporting sentences.

Each group of items below includes one topic, one main idea (expressed in a topic sentence), and two supporting details for that idea. In the space provided, label each item with one of the following:

Activity

3

> *T* — topic
> *MI* — main idea
> *SD* — supporting details

1. _____ a. The weather in the summer is often hot and sticky.

   _____ b. Summer can be an unpleasant time of year.

   _____ c. Summer.

   _____ d. Bug bites, poison ivy, and allergies are a big part of summertime.

2. _____ a. The new Ultimate sports car is bound to be very popular.

   _____ b. The company has promised to provide any repairs needed during the first three years at no charge.

   _____ c. Because it gets thirty miles per gallon of gas, it offers real savings on fuel costs.

   _____ d. The new Ultimate sports car.

3. _____ a. Decorating an apartment doesn't need to be expensive.

   _____ b. A few plants add a touch of color without costing a lot of money.

   _____ c. Inexpensive braided rugs can be bought to match nearly any furniture.

   _____ d. Decorating an apartment.

4. _____ a. Long practice sessions and busy game schedules take too much time away from schoolwork.

   _____ b. High school sports.

   _____ c. The competition between schools may become so intense that, depending on the outcome of one game, athletes are either adored or scorned.

   _____ d. High school sports put too much pressure on young athletes.

5. _____ a. After mapping out the best route to your destination, phone ahead for motel reservations.

   _____ b. A long car trip.

   _____ c. Following a few guidelines before a long car trip can help you avoid potential problems.

   _____ d. Have your car's engine tuned as well, and have the tires, brakes, and exhaust system inspected.

Activities in Goal 2: Support the Point

www.mhhe.com/langan

Effective writing gives support—reasons, facts, examples, and other evidence—for each main point. While main points are general (see page 15), support is *specific;* it provides the details that explain the main point.

   To write well, you must know the difference between general and specific ideas. It is helpful to realize that you use general and specific ideas all the time in your everyday life. For example, in choosing a DVD to rent, you may think, "Which should I rent, an action movie, a comedy, or a romance?" In such a case, *DVD* is the general idea, and *action movie, comedy,* and *romance* are the specific ideas.

Recognizing Specific Details

Specific details are examples, reasons, particulars, and facts. Such details are needed to support and explain a topic sentence effectively. They provide the evidence needed for us to understand, as well as to feel and experience, a writer's point.

Below is a topic sentence followed by two sets of supporting sentences. Put a check mark next to the set that provides sharp, specific details.

Topic sentence: Ticket sales for a recent U2 concert proved that the rock band is still very popular.

_____ a. Fans came from everywhere to buy tickets to the concert. People wanted good seats and were willing to endure a great deal of various kinds of discomfort as they waited in line for many hours. Some people actually waited for days, sleeping at night in uncomfortable circumstances. Good tickets were sold out extremely quickly.

_____ b. The first person in the long ticket line spent three days standing in the hot sun and three nights sleeping on the concrete without even a pillow. The man behind her waited equally long in his wheelchair. The ticket window opened at 10:00 A.M, and the tickets for the good seats—those in front of the stage—were sold out an hour later.

EXPLANATION The second set (*b*) provides specific details. Instead of a vague statement about fans who were "willing to endure a great deal of various kinds of discomforts," we get vivid details we can see and picture clearly: "three days standing in the hot sun," "three nights sleeping on the concrete without even a pillow," "The man behind her waited equally long in his wheelchair."

Instead of a vague statement that tickets were "sold out extremely quickly," we get exact and vivid details: "The ticket window opened at 10:00 A.M., and the tickets for the good seats—those in front of the stage—were sold out an hour later."

Specific details are often like a movie script. They provide us with such clear pictures that we could make a film of them if we wanted to. You would know just how to film the information given in the second set of sentences. You would show the fans in line under a hot sun and, later, sleeping on the concrete. The first person in line would be shown sleeping without a pillow under her head. You would show tickets finally going on sale, and after an hour you could show the ticket seller explaining that all the seats in front of the stage were sold out.

continued

In contrast, the writer of the first set of sentences (*a*) fails to provide the specific information needed. If you were asked to make a film based on set *a*, you would have to figure out on your own just what particulars to show.

When you are working to provide specific supporting information in a paper, it might help to ask yourself, "Could someone easily film this information?" If the answer is yes, your supporting details are specific enough for your readers to visualize.

Activity 8

Each topic sentence below is followed by two sets of supporting details. Write *S* (for *specific*) in the space next to the set that provides specific support for the point. Write *G* (for *general*) next to the set that offers only vague, general support.

> **HINT** Which set of supporting details could you more readily use in a film?

1. *Topic sentence:* The West Side shopping mall is an unpleasant place.

    _____ a. The floors are covered with cigarette butts, dirty paper plates, and spilled food. The stores are so crowded I had to wait twenty minutes just to get a dressing room to try on a shirt.

    _____ b. It's very dirty, and not enough places are provided for trash. The stores are not equipped to handle the large number of shoppers that often show up.

2. *Topic sentence:* Our golden retriever is a wonderful pet for children.

    _____ a. He is gentle, patient, eager to please, and affectionate. Capable of following orders, he is also ready to think for himself and find solutions to a problem. He senses children's moods and goes along with their wishes.

    _____ b. He doesn't bite, even when children pull his tail. After learning to catch a ball, he will bring it back again and again, seemingly always ready to play. If the children don't want to play anymore, he will just sit by their side, gazing at them with his faithful eyes.

3. *Topic sentence:* My two-year-old daughter's fearlessness is a constant source of danger to her.

    _____ a. She doesn't realize that certain activities are dangerous. Even when I warn her, she will go ahead and do something that could hurt her. I have to constantly be on the lookout for dangerous situations and try to protect her from them.

_____ b. For instance, she loves going to the swimming pool. That's great. But she will jump into water that is way over her head. She likes animals and will run to pet any dog that wanders by, no matter how unfriendly.

4. *Topic sentence:* People's views of scientists are often more fiction than fact.

_____ a. Scientists are portrayed in movies as crazy guys with long hair, thick glasses, and shabby clothes. Incapable of remembering the time of day, these imaginary scientists skip meals and prefer the company of laboratory animals to that of their own children. In reality, scientists get hungry at mealtime, love their children, and go to work in suits.

_____ b. People don't know exactly what scientists do and fantasize a lot about their work. Instead of thinking of scientists as real people who do a particular type of work, people think of them as weird, antisocial geniuses whom one could spot a mile away. In reality, most scientists look and act much like their neighbors.

5. *Topic sentence:* Early theories of child raising were very different from today's theories.

_____ a. The first books on child raising came out hundreds of years ago. The advice they contained was based almost entirely on superstitions and other untrue beliefs. Some of the advice was harmless, but some could lead to long-term effects. They told parents to do things to their children that seem to us to make no sense at all.

_____ b. One early book, for example, advised mothers not to breast-feed their babies right after feeling anger because the anger would go into the milk and injure the child. Another told parents to begin toilet training their children at the age of three weeks and to tie their babies' arms down for several months to prevent thumb sucking.

At several points in each of the following paragraphs, you are given a choice of two sets of supporting details. Write *S* (for *specific*) in the space next to the set that provides specific support for the point. Write *G* (for *general*) next to the set that offers only vague, general support.

Activity

9

Paragraph 1
My daughter is as shy as I am, and it breaks my heart to see her dealing with the same problems I had to deal with in my childhood because of my shyness. I feel very sad for her when I see the problems she has making friends.

_____ a. It takes her a long time to begin to do the things other children do to make friends, and her feelings get hurt very easily over one thing and another. She is not at all comfortable about making connections with her classmates at school.

_____ b. She usually spends Christmas vacation alone because by that time of year she doesn't have friends yet. Only when her birthday comes in the summer is she confident enough to invite school friends to her party. Once she sends out the invitations, she almost sleeps by the telephone, waiting for the children to respond. If they say they can't come, her eyes fill with tears.

I recognize very well her signs of shyness, which make her look smaller and more fragile than she really is.

_____ c. When she has to talk to someone she doesn't know well, she speaks in a whisper and stares sideways. Pressing her hands together, she lifts her shoulders as though she wished she could hide her head between them.

_____ d. When she is forced to talk to anyone other than her family and her closest friends, the sound of her voice and the position of her head change. Even her posture changes in a way that makes it look as if she's trying to make her body disappear.

It is hard for me to watch her passing unnoticed at school.

_____ e. She never gets chosen for a special job or privilege, even though she tries her best, practicing in privacy at home. She just doesn't measure up. Worst of all, even her teacher seems to forget her existence much of the time.

_____ f. Although she rehearses in our basement, she never gets chosen for a good part in a play. Her voice is never loud or clear enough. Worst of all, her teacher doesn't call on her in class for days at a time.

Paragraph 2

It is said that the dog is man's best friend, but I strongly believe that the honor belongs to my computer. A computer won't fetch a stick for me, but it can help me entertain myself in many ways.

_____ a. If I am bored, tired, or out of ideas, the computer allows me to explore things that interest me such as anything relating to the world of professional sports.

_____ b. The other day, I used my computer to visit the National Football League's Web site. I was then able to get injury updates for players on my favorite team, the Philadelphia Eagles.

While the dog is a faithful friend, it does not allow me to be a more responsible person the way my computer does.

_____ c. I use my computer to pay all my bills automatically over the Internet. I also use it to balance my checkbook and keep track of my expenses. Now I always know how much money is in my account at the end of the month.

_____ d. The computer helps me be responsible with financial matters because it records my transactions. With the computer I have access to more information, which allows me to make good decisions with my money.

A dog might help me meet strangers I see in the park, but the computer helps me meet people who share my interests.

_____ e. With my computer, I can go online and find people with every type of hobby or interest. Thousands of online chat rooms and discussion groups are available featuring people from all over the country—and the world. The computer can even allow me to develop meaningful personal relationships with others.

_____ f. Two months ago, I discovered a Web site for people in my community who enjoy hiking. I'm planning to meet a group next Saturday for a day hike. And earlier this year, I met my wonderful fiancée, Shelly, through a computer dating service.

Providing Specific Details

Each of the following sentences contains a general word or words, set off in _italic_ type. Substitute sharp, specific words in each case.

EXAMPLE

After the parade, the city street was littered with _garbage_.

After the parade, the city street was littered with multicolored confetti, dirty popcorn, and lifeless balloons.

Activity

10

1. If I had enough money, I'd visit *several places*.

   _____

   _____

2. It took her *a long time* to get home.

   _____

   _____

3. Ron is often stared at because of his *unusual hair color and hairstyle*.

   _____

   _____

4. After you pass *two buildings*, you'll see my house on the left.

   _____

   _____

5. Nia's purse is crammed with *lots of stuff*.

   _____

   _____

6. I bought *some junk food* for the long car trip.

   _____

   _____

7. The floor in the front of my car is covered with *things*.

   _____

   _____

8. When his mother said no to his request for a toy, the child *reacted strongly*.

   _____

   _____

9. Devan gave his girlfriend a *surprise present* for Valentine's Day.

   _____

   _____

10. My cat can *do a wonderful trick*.

   _____

   _____

Selecting Details That Fit

The details in your paper must all clearly relate to and support your opening point. If a detail does not support your point, leave it out. Otherwise, your paper will lack unity. For example, see if you can circle the letters of the two sentences that do *not* support the topic sentence below.

> *Topic sentence:* Mario is a very talented person.
> a. Mario is always courteous to his professors.
> b. He has created beautiful paintings in his art course.
> c. Mario is the lead singer in a local band.
> d. He won an award in a photography contest.
> e. He is hoping to become a professional photographer.

> **EXPLANATION**   Being courteous may be a virtue, but it is not a talent, so sentence *a* does not support the topic sentence. Also, Mario's desire to become a professional photographer tells us nothing about his talent; thus sentence *e* does not support the topic sentence either. The other three statements all clearly back up the topic sentence. Each in some way supports the idea that Mario is talented—in art, as a singer, or as a photographer.

In each group below, circle the two items that do *not* support the topic sentence.

1. *Topic sentence:* Carla seems attracted only to men who are unavailable.
   a. She once fell in love with a man serving a life sentence in prison.
   b. Her parents worry about her inability to connect with a nice single man.
   c. She wants to get married and have kids before she is thirty.
   d. Her current boyfriend is married.
   e. Recently she had a huge crush on a movie star.

2. *Topic sentence:* Some dog owners have little consideration for other people.
   a. Obedience lessons can be a good experience for both the dog and the owner.
   b. Some dog owners let their dogs leave droppings on the sidewalk or in other people's yards.
   c. They leave the dog home alone for hours, barking and howling and waking the neighbors.
   d. Some people keep very large dogs in small apartments.
   e. Even when small children are playing nearby, they let their bad-tempered dogs run loose.

Activity

11

3. *Topic sentence:* Dr. Eliot is not a good teacher.
    a. He cancels class frequently with no explanation.
    b. When a student asks a question that he can't answer, he becomes irritated with the student.
    c. He got his Ph.D at a university in another country.
    d. He's taught at the college for many years and is on a number of faculty committees.
    e. He puts off grading papers until the end of the semester and then returns them all at once.

4. *Topic sentence:* Some doctors seem to think it is all right to keep patients waiting.
    a. Pharmaceutical sales representatives sometimes must wait hours to see a doctor.
    b. The doctors stand in the hallway chatting with nurses and secretaries even when they have a waiting room full of patients.
    c. Patients sometimes travel long distances to consult with a particular doctor.
    d. When a patient calls before an appointment to see if the doctor is on time, the answer is often yes even when the doctor is two hours behind schedule.
    e. Some doctors schedule appointments in a way that ensures long lines, to make it appear that they are especially skillful.

5. *Topic sentence:* Several factors were responsible for the staggering loss of lives when the *Titanic* sank.
    a. Over 1,500 people died in the *Titanic* disaster; only 711 survived.
    b. Despite warnings about the presence of icebergs, the captain allowed the *Titanic* to continue at high speed.
    c. If the ship had hit the iceberg head on, its watertight compartments might have kept it from sinking; however, it hit on the side, resulting in a long, jagged gash through which water poured in.
    d. The *Titanic,* equipped with the very best communication systems available in 1912, sent out SOS messages.
    e. When the captain gave orders to abandon the *Titanic,* many passengers refused because they believed the ship was unsinkable, so many lifeboats were only partly filled.

Understanding Transitions

Transitions are words and phrases that indicate relationships between ideas. They are like signposts that guide travelers, showing them how to move smoothly from one spot to the next. Be sure to take advantage of transitions. They will help organize and connect your ideas, and they will help your readers follow the direction of your thoughts.

To see how transitions help, write a check beside the item in each pair that is easier to read and understand.

Pair A

_____ One way to stay in shape is to eat low-calorie, low-fat foods. A good strategy is to walk or jog at least twenty minutes four times a week.

_____ One way to stay in shape is to eat low-calorie, low-fat foods. Another good strategy is to walk or jog at least twenty minutes four times a week.

Pair B

_____ I begin each study session by going to a quiet place and setting out my textbook, pen, and notebook. I check my assignment book to see what I have to read.

_____ I begin each study session by going to a quiet place and setting out my textbook, pen, and notebook. Then I check my assignment book to see what I have to read.

> **EXPLANATION** In each pair, the second item is easier to read and understand. In pair A, the listing word *another* makes it clear that the writer is going on to a second way to stay in shape. In pair B, the time word *then* makes the relationship between the sentences clear. The writer first sets out the textbook and a pen and notebook and *then* checks an assignment book to see what to do.

Using Transitions

As already stated, transitions are signal words that help readers follow the direction of the writer's thought. To see the value of transitions, look at the two versions of the short paragraph below. Check the version that is easier to read and understand.

_____ a. Where will you get the material for your writing assignments? There are several good sources. Your own experience is a major resource. For an assignment about childhood, for instance, you can draw on your own numerous memories of childhood. Other people's experience is extremely useful. You may have heard people you know or even people on TV or radio talking about their childhood. Or you can interview people with a specific writing assignment in mind. Books and magazines are a good source of material for assignments. Many experts, for example, have written about various aspects of childhood.

_____ b. Where will you get the material for your writing assignments? There are several good sources. First of all, your own experience is a major resource. For an assignment about childhood, for instance, you can draw on your own numerous memories of childhood. In addition, other people's experiences are extremely useful. You may have heard people you know or even people on TV or radio talking about their childhood. Or you can interview people with a specific writing assignment in mind. Finally, books and magazines are a good source of material for assignments. Many experts, for example, have written about various aspects of childhood.

EXPLANATION   You no doubt chose the second version, *b*. The listing transitions—*first of all, in addition,* and *finally*—make it clear when the author is introducing a new supporting point. The reader of paragraph *b* is better able to follow the author's line of thinking and to note that three main sources of material for assignments are being listed: your own experience, other people's experience, and books and magazines.

Activity

15

The following paragraphs use listing order or time order. In each case, fill in the blanks with appropriate transitions from the box above the paragraph. Use each transition once.

1.

after   now   first   soon   while

My husband has developed an interesting hobby, in which I, unfortunately, am unable to share. He _____ enrolled in ground flight instruction classes at the local community college. The lessons were all about air safety regulations and procedures. _____ passing a difficult exam, he decided to take flying lessons at the city airport. Every Monday he would wake at six o'clock in the morning and drive happily to the airport, eager to see his instructor. _____ he was taking lessons, he started to buy airplane magazines and talk about them constantly. "Look at that Cessna 150," he would say. "Isn't she a beauty?" _____, after many lessons, he is flying by himself. _____ he will be able to carry passengers. That is my biggest nightmare. I know he will want me to fly with him, but I am not a lover of heights. I can't understand why someone would leave the safety of the ground to be in the sky, defense- less as a kite.

2. | **finally   for one thing   second** |

The karate class I took last week convinced me that martial arts may never be my strong point. _____, there is the issue of balance. The instructor asked everyone in class to stand on one foot to practice kicking. Each time I tired, I wobbled and had to spread my arms out wide to avoid falling. I even stumbled into Mr. Kim, my instructor, who glared at me. _____, there was the issue of flexibility. Mr. Kim asked us to stretch and touch our toes. Everyone did this without a problem—except me. I could barely reach my knees before pain raced up and down my back. _____, there was my lack of coordination. When everyone started practicing blocks, I got confused. I couldn't figure out where to move my arms and legs. By the time I got the first move right, the whole group had finished three more. By the end of my first lesson, I was completely lost.

3. | **later   soon   when   then** |

At the age of thirty-one I finally had the opportunity to see snow for the first time in my life. It was in New York City on a cloudy afternoon in November. My daughter and I had gone to the American Museum of Natural History. _____ we left the museum, snow was falling gently. I thought that it was so beauti- ful! It made me remember movies I had seen countless times in my native Brazil. We decided to find a taxi. _____ we were crossing Central Park, snuggled in the cozy cab, watching the snow cover trees, bushes, branches, and grass. We were amazed to see the landscape quickly change from fall to winter. _____ we arrived in front of our hotel, and I still remember stepping on the crisp snow and laughing like a child who is touched by magic. _____ that day, I heard on the radio that another snowstorm was coming. I was naive enough to wait for thunder and the other sounds of a rainstorm. I did not know yet that snow, even a snowstorm, is silent and soft.

4. | **last of all   another   first of all   in addition** |

Public school students who expect to attend school from September to June, and then have a long summer vacation, may be in for a big surprise before long. For a number of reasons, many schools are switching to a year-round calendar. _____, many educators point out that the traditional school calendar was established years ago when young people had to be available during the summer months to work on farms, but this necessity has long since passed. _____ reason is that a longer school year accommodates individual learning rates more effectively. That is, fast learners can go into more depth about a subject that interests them, while those who learn at a slower pace have more time to master the essential material. _____, many communities have gone to year-round school to relieve overcrowding, since students can be put on different schedules throughout the year. _____, and perhaps most important, educators feel that year-round schools eliminate the loss of learning that many students experience over a long summer break.

Organizing Details in a Paragraph

The supporting details in a paragraph must be organized in a meaningful way. The two most common methods of organizing details are listing order and time order. The activities that follow will give you practice in both methods of organization.

Use *listing order* to arrange the scrambled list of sentences below. Number each supporting sentence 1, 2, 3,... so that you go from the least important item to what is presented as the most important item.

Note that transitions will help by making clear the relationships between some of the sentences.

Activity

16

Topic sentence: I am no longer a big fan of professional sports, for a number of reasons.

_____ Basketball and hockey continue well into the baseball season, and football doesn't have its Super Bowl until the middle of winter, when basketball should be at center stage.

_____ In addition, I detest the high fives, taunting, and trash talk that so many professional athletes now indulge in during games.

_____ Second, I am bothered by the length of professional sports seasons.

_____ Also, professional athletes have no loyalty to a team or city as they greedily sell their abilities to the highest bidder.

_____ For one thing, greed is the engine running professional sports.

_____ There are numerous news stories of professional athletes in trouble with the law because of drugs, guns, fights, traffic accidents, or domestic violence.

_____ After a good year, athletes making millions become unhappy if they aren't rewarded with a new contract calling for even more millions.

_____ But the main reason I've become disenchanted with professional sports is the disgusting behavior of so many of its performers.

Use *time order* to arrange the scrambled sentences below. Number the supporting sentences in the order in which they occur in time (1, 2, 3,...).

Note that transitions will help by making clear the relationships between sentences.

Activity

17

Topic sentence: If you are a smoker, the following steps should help you quit.

_____ Before your "quit day" arrives, have a medical checkup to make sure it will be all right for you to begin an exercise program.

_____ You should then write down on a card your decision to quit and the date of your "quit day."

_____ When your "quit day" arrives, stop smoking and start your exercise program.

_____ Finally, remind yourself repeatedly how good you will feel when you can confidently tell yourself and others that you are a nonsmoker.

_____ Place the card in a location where you will be sure to see it every day.

_____ When you begin this exercise program, be sure to drink plenty of water every day and to follow a sensible diet.

_____ After making a definite decision to stop smoking, select a specific "quit day."

_____ Eventually, your exercise program should include activities strenuous enough to strengthen your lung capacity and your overall stamina.

Activities in Goal 4: Write Error-Free Sentences

www.mhhe.com/langan

Effective writing is free of errors that distract or confuse readers. Whether you are writing a paragraph, letter, job application, or resume, you must learn to write clear, error-free sentences. The activities in Part Two of this book will help you do just that.

The Writing Process

3

Steps in the Writing Process

Even professional writers do not sit down and write a paper automatically, in one draft. Instead, they have to work on it a step at a time. Writing a paper is a process that can be divided into the following steps:

- *Step 1:* Getting Started through Prewriting
- *Step 2:* Preparing a Scratch Outline
- *Step 3*: Writing the First Draft
- *Step 4:* Revising
- *Step 5:* Editing and Proofreading

These steps are described on the following pages.

Step 1: Getting Started through Prewriting

What you need to learn first are strategies for working on a paper. These strategies will help you do the thinking needed to figure out both the point you want to make and the support you have for that point.

There are several *prewriting strategies*—strategies you use before writing the first draft of your paper:

- Freewriting
- Questioning
- Clustering
- Making a list

Freewriting

Freewriting is just sitting down and writing whatever comes into your mind about a topic. Do this for ten minutes or so. Write without stopping and without worrying at all about spelling, grammar, or the like. Simply get down on paper all the information about the topic that occurs to you.

Here is the freewriting Gary did on his problems with returning to school. Gary had been given the assignment "Write about a problem you are facing at the present time." Gary felt right away that he could write about his college situation. He began prewriting as a way to explore and generate details on his topic.

EXAMPLE OF FREEWRITING

One thing I want to write about is going back to school. At age twenty-nine. A lot to deal with. I sometimes wonder if Im nuts to try to do this or just stupid. I had to deal with my folks when I decided. My dad hated school. He knew when to quit, I'll say that for him. But he doesn't understand Im different. I have a right to my own life. And I want to better myself. He teases me alot. Says things like didnt you get dumped on enough in high school, why go back for more. My mom doesnt understand either. Just keeps worring about where the money was coming from. Then my friends. They make fun of me. Also my wife has to do more of the heavy house stuff because I'm out so much. Getting back to my friends, they say dumb things to get my goat. Like calling me the college man or saying ooh, we'd better watch our grammer. Sometimes I think my dads right, school was no fun for me. Spent years just sitting in class waiting for final bell so I could escape. Teachers didnt help me or take an intrest, some of them made me feel like a real loser. Now things are different and I like most of my teachers. I can talk to the teacher after class or to ask questions if I'm confused. But I really need more time to spend with family, I hardly see them any more. What I am doing is hard all round for them and me.

What electronic devices do you consider essential to your everyday life? What electronic devices could you live without? On a separate piece of paper, freewrite for several minutes on what you would do if you could not use one of your essential electronic devices, such as a cell phone, for a week.

Notice that there are problems with spelling, grammar, and punctuation in Gary's freewriting. Gary is not worried about such matters, nor should he be. He is just concentrating on getting ideas and details down on paper. He knows that it is best to focus on one thing at a time. At this stage, he just wants to write out thoughts as they come to him, to do some thinking on paper.

You should take the same approach when freewriting: explore your topic without worrying at all about being "correct." At this early stage of the writing process, focus all your attention on figuring out what you want to say.

Questioning

Questioning means that you think about your topic by writing down a series of questions and answers about it. Your questions can start with words like *what, when, where, why,* and *how.*

Here are some questions that Gary might have asked while developing his paper, as well as some answers to those questions.

www.mhhe.com/langan

EXAMPLE OF QUESTIONING

Why do I have a problem with returning to school?	My parents and friends don't support me.
How do they not support me?	Dad asks why I want to be dumped on more. Mom is upset because college costs lots of money. Friends tease me about being a college man.
When do they not support me?	When I go to my parents' home for Friday night visits, when my friends see me walking toward them.
Where do I have this problem?	At home, where I barely see my wife and daughter before having to go to class, and where I have to let my wife do house things on weekends while I'm studying.
Why else do I have this problem?	High school was bad experience.
What details back up the idea that high school was bad experience?	Sat in class bored, couldn't wait to get out, teachers didn't help me. One embarrassed me when I didn't know the answer.

Clustering

Clustering is another prewriting strategy that can be used to generate material for a paper. It is helpful for people who like to do their thinking in a visual way.

In *clustering,* you begin by stating your subject in a few words in the center of a blank sheet of paper. Then as ideas come to you, put them in ovals, boxes, or circles around the subject, and draw lines to connect them to the subject. Put minor ideas or details in smaller boxes or circles, and also use connecting lines to show how they relate.

Keep in mind that there is no right or wrong way of clustering. It is a way to think on paper about how various ideas and details relate to one another. Below is an example of clustering that Gary might have done to develop his idea.

EXAMPLE OF CLUSTERING

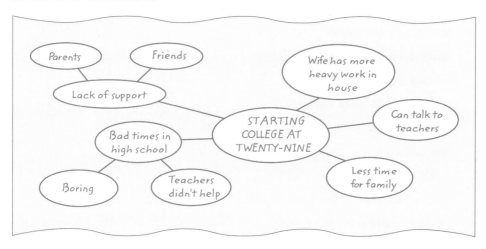

Making a List

In *making a list*—a prewriting strategy also known as *listing, list making,* and *brainstorming*—you make a list of ideas and details that could go into your paper. Simply pile these items up, one after another, without worrying about putting them in any special order. Try to accumulate as many details as you can think of.

After Gary did his freewriting about returning to school, he made up the list of details shown below.

EXAMPLE OF LISTING

> parents give me hard time when they see me
>
> Dad hated school
>
> Dad quit school after eighth grade
>
> Dad says I was dumped on enough in high school
>
> Dad asks why I want to go back for more
>
> Mom also doesnt understand

continued

keeps asking how Ill pay for it

friends give me a hard time too

friends call me college man

say they have to watch their grammar

my wife has more heavy work around the house

also high school had been no fun for me

just sat in class after class

couldnt wait for final bell to ring

wanted to escape

teachers didnt help me

teachers didnt take an interest in me

one called on me, then told me to forget it

I felt like a real loser

I didnt want to go back to his class

now I'm more sure of myself

OK not to know an answer

talk to teachers after class

job plus schoolwork take all my time

get home late, then rush through dinner

then spend evening studying

even have to do homework on weekends

One detail led to another as Gary expanded his list. Slowly but surely, more supporting material emerged that he could use in developing his paper. By the time he had finished his list, he was ready to plan an outline of his paragraph and to write his first draft.

Notice that in making a list, as in freewriting, details are included that will not actually end up in the final paragraph. Gary decided later not to develop the idea that his wife now has more heavy work to do in the house. And he realized that several of his details were about why school is easier in college ("now I'm more sure of myself," "OK not to know an answer," and "talk to instructors after class"); such details were not relevant to his point.

Once you have decided on the goal you wish to write about, write a topic sentence about it such as any of the following:

- After several false starts, I finally quite smoking.
- After gradually changing my attitude about school, I have begun to get good grades.
- Following a careful budget, I was finally able to afford to . . .

PART 2

Sentence Skills

Introduction

Part Two explains the basic skills needed to write clear, error-free sentences. While the skills are presented within five traditional categories (sentences; verbs, pronouns, and agreement; modifiers and parallelism; punctuation and mechanics; word use), each section is self-contained so that you can go directly to the skills you need to work on. Note, however, that you may find it helpful to cover Chapter 4, "Subjects and Verbs," before turning to other skills. Typically, the main features of a skill are presented on the first pages of a section; secondary points are developed later. Numerous activities are provided so that you can practice skills enough to make them habits. The activities are varied and range from underlining answers to writing complete sentences involving the skill in question. One or more review tests at the end of each section offer additional practice activities. Mastery tests conclude each chapter, allowing you to immediately test your understanding of each skill.

What are your plans for the future after you have graduated from college? What five things would you like to do as a result of graduating from college? On a separate piece of paper, using any of the prewriting techniques discussed so far (freewriting, questioning, clustering, making a list), spend time prewriting for a paper on your plans for the future after college.

Subjects and Verbs

4

Introductory Activity

Understanding subjects and verbs is a big step toward mastering many sentence skills. As a speaker of English, you already have an instinctive feel for these **basic building blocks of English sentences.** See if you can insert an appropriate word in each space below. The answer will be a subject.

1. The _____ will soon be over.

2. _____ cannot be trusted.

3. A strange _____ appeared in my backyard.

4. _____ is one of my favorite activities.

Now insert an appropriate word in the following spaces. Each answer will be a verb.

5. The prisoner _____ at the judge.

6. My sister _____ much harder than I do.

7. The players _____ in the locker room.

8. Rob and Marilyn _____ with the teacher.

Finally, insert appropriate words in the following spaces. Each answer will be a subject in the first space and a verb in the second.

9. The _____ almost _____ out of the tree.

10. Many _____ today _____ sex and violence.

11. The _____ carefully _____ the patient.

12. A _____ quickly _____ the ball.

The basic building blocks of English sentences are subjects and verbs. Understanding them is an important first step toward mastering a number of sentence skills.

Every sentence has a subject and a verb. Who or what the sentence speaks about is called the *subject;* what the sentence says about the subject is called the *verb.* In the following sentences, the subject is underlined once and the verb twice:

1. People gossip.

2. The truck belched fumes.

3. He waved at me.

4. Alaska contains the largest wilderness area in the United States.

5. That woman is a millionaire.

6. The pants feel itchy.

A Simple Way to Find a Subject

To find a subject, ask *who* or *what* the sentence is about. As shown below, your answer is the subject.

Who is the first sentence about? People

What is the second sentence about? The truck

Who is the third sentence about? He

What is the fourth sentence about? Alaska

Who is the fifth sentence about? That woman

What is the sixth sentence about? The pants

It helps to remember that the subject of a sentence is always a *noun* (any person, place, or thing) or a pronoun. A *pronoun* is simply a word like *he, she, it, you,* or *they* used in place of a noun. In the preceding sentences, the subjects are persons (*People, He, woman*), a place (*Alaska*), and things (*truck, pants*). And note that one pronoun (*He*) is used as a subject.

A Simple Way to Find a Verb

To find a verb, ask what the sentence *says* about the subject. As shown below, your answer is the verb.

What does the first sentence *say about* people? They gossip.

What does the second sentence *say about* the truck? It belched (fumes).

What does the third sentence *say about* him? He waved (at me).

What does the fourth sentence *say about* Alaska? It contains (the largest wilderness area in the United States).

What does the fifth sentence *say about* that woman? She is (a millionaire).

What does the sixth sentence *say about* the pants? They feel (itchy).

A second way to find the verb is to put *I, you, he, she, it,* or *they* in front of the word you think is a verb. If the result makes sense, you have a verb. For example, you could put *they* in front of *gossip* in the first sentence above, with the result, *they gossip,* making sense. Therefore, you know that *gossip* is a verb. You could use the same test with the other verbs as well.

Finally, it helps to remember that most verbs show action. In "People gossip," the action is gossiping. In "The truck belched fumes," the action is belching. In "He waved at me," the action is waving. In "Alaska contains the largest wilderness area in the United States," the action is containing.

Certain other verbs, known as *linking verbs,* do not show action. They do, however, give information about the subject of the sentence. In "That woman is a millionaire," the linking verb *is* tells us that the woman is a millionaire. In "The pants feel itchy," the linking verb *feel* gives us the information that the pants are itchy.

Practice

1

In each of the following sentences, draw one line under the subject and two lines under the verb.

To find the subject, ask *who* or *what* the sentence is about. Then, to find the verb, ask what the sentence *says about* the subject.

1. I ate an entire pizza by myself.

2. Alligators swim in that lake.

3. April failed the test.

4. The television movie ended suddenly.

5. Keiko borrowed change for the pay telephone.

6. The children stared in wide-eyed wonderment at the Thanksgiving Day floats.

7. An old newspaper tumbled down the dirty street.

8. Lola starts every morning with a series of yoga exercises.

9. My part-time job limits my study time.

10. The windstorm blew over the storage shed in the backyard.

Follow the directions given for Practice 1. Note that all of the verbs here are linking verbs.

Practice 2

1. My sister is a terrible speller.

2. Potato chips are Ramon's favorite snack.

3. The defendant appeared very nervous on the witness stand.

4. Art became a father at the age of twenty.

5. The ride going somewhere always seems longer than the ride coming back.

6. That apartment building was an abandoned factory two years ago.

7. My first two weeks on the sales job were the worst of my life.

8. The plastic banana split and Styrofoam birthday cake in the bakery window look like real desserts.

9. Jane always feels energized after a cup of coffee.

10. Rooms with white walls seem larger than those with dark-colored walls.

Follow the directions given for Practice 1.

Practice 3

1. That clock runs about five minutes fast.

2. The new player on the team is much too sure of himself.

3. Late-afternoon shoppers filled the aisles of the supermarket.

4. Garbage trucks rumbled down my street on their way to the dump.

5. The children drew pictures on the steamed window.

6. The picture fell suddenly to the floor.

7. Chipmunks live in the woodpile behind my house.

8. Our loud uncle monopolized the conversation at the dinner table.

9. The tomatoes were soft to the touch.

10. The insurance company canceled my policy because of a speeding ticket.

www.mhhe.com/langan

More about Subjects and Verbs

Distinguishing Subjects from Prepositional Phrases

The subject of a sentence never appears within a prepositional phrase. A *prepositional phrase* is simply a group of words beginning with a preposition and ending with the answer to the question *what, when,* or *where.* Here is a list of common prepositions.

Common Prepositions				
about	before	by	inside	over
above	behind	during	into	through
across	below	except	of	to
among	beneath	for	off	toward
around	beside	from	on	under
at	between	in	onto	with

When you are looking for the subject of a sentence, it is helpful to cross out prepositional phrases.

In the middle of the night, we heard footsteps on the roof.

The magazines on the table belong in the garage.

Before the opening kickoff, a brass band marched onto the field.

The hardware store across the street went out of business.

In spite of our advice, Sally quit her job at Burger King.

Practice

4

Cross out prepositional phrases. Then draw a single line under subjects and a double line under verbs.

1. For that course, you need three different books.

2. The key to the front door slipped from my hand into a puddle.

3. The checkout lines at the supermarket moved very slowly.

4. With his son, Jamal walked to the playground.

5. No quarrel between good friends lasts for a very long time.

6. In one weekend, Martha planted a large vegetable garden in her backyard.

7. Either of my brothers is a reliable worker.

8. The drawer of the bureau sticks on rainy days.

9. During the movie, several people walked out in protest.

10. At a single sitting, my brother reads five or more comic books.

Verbs of More Than One Word

Many verbs consist of more than one word. Here, for example, are some of the many forms of the verb *help:*

Some Forms of the Verb *Help*

helps	should have been helping	will have helped
helping	can help	would have been helped
is helping	would have been helping	has been helped
was helping	will be helping	had been helped
may help	had been helping	must have helped
should help	helped	having helped
will help	have helped	should have been helped
does help	has helped	had helped

Below are sentences that contain verbs of more than one word:

Yolanda is working overtime this week.

Another book has been written about the Kennedy family.

We should have stopped for gas at the last station.

The game has just been canceled.

TIPS

1. Words like *not, just, never, only,* and *always* are not part of the verb, although they may appear within the verb.

    Yolanda is not working overtime next week.

    The boys should just not have stayed out so late.

    The game has always been played regardless of the weather.

2. No verb preceded by *to* is ever the verb of a sentence.

    Sue wants to go with us.

    The newly married couple decided to rent a house for a year.

    The store needs extra people to help out at Christmas.

3. No *-ing* word by itself is ever the verb of a sentence. (It may be part of the verb, but it must have a helping verb in front of it.)

    We planning the trip for months. (This is not a sentence, because the verb is not complete.)

    We were planning the trip for months. (This is a complete sentence.)

Practice

5

Draw a single line under subjects and a double line under verbs. Be sure to include all parts of the verb.

1. He has been sleeping all day.

2. The wood foundations of the shed were attacked by termites.

3. I have not washed my car for several months.

4. The instructor had not warned us about the quiz.

5. The bus will be leaving shortly.

6. You should not try to pet that temperamental hamster.

7. They have just been married by a justice of the peace.

8. He could make a living with his wood carvings.

9. Kim has decided to ask her boss for a raise.

10. The employees should have warned us about the wet floor.

Compound Subjects and Verbs

A sentence may have more than one verb:

The dancer stumbled and fell.

Lola washed her hair, blew it dry, and parted it in the middle.

A sentence may have more than one subject:

Cats and dogs are sometimes the best of friends.

The striking workers and their bosses could not come to an agreement.

A sentence may have several subjects and several verbs:

Holly and I read the book and reported on it to the class.

Pete, Nick, and Eric caught the fish in the morning, cleaned them in the after-

noon, and ate them that night.

Draw a single line under subjects and a double line under verbs. Be sure to mark *all* the subjects and verbs.

Practice

6

1. The hypnotist locked his assistant in a box and sawed her in half.

2. Trina began her paper at 7:30 and finished it at midnight.

3. On the shipping pier, the Nissans, Toyotas, and Hondas glittered in the sun.

4. Tony added the column of figures three times and got three different totals.

5. The car sputtered, stalled, and then started again.

6. Whiteflies, mites, and aphids infected my houseplants.

7. Rosa disconnected the computers and carried them to her car.

8. We walked over to the corner deli and bought extra cheese for the party.

9. At the new shopping mall, Tony and Lola looked in windows for two hours

   and then bought one pair of socks.

10. My aunt and uncle married in their twenties, divorced in their thirties, and

    then remarried in their forties.

Review Test 1

Draw one line under the subjects and two lines under the verbs. As necessary, cross out prepositional phrases to help find subjects. Underline all the parts of a verb. And remember that you may find more than one subject and verb in a sentence.

1. I had not heard about the cancellation of the class.

2. James should have gotten an estimate from the plumber.

3. The family played badminton and volleyball at the picnic.

4. A solution to the problem popped suddenly into my head.

5. My roommate and I will need to study all night for the test.

6. Chang has not been eating in the cafeteria this semester.

7. The white moon hung above the castle like a grinning skull.

8. Len and Marie drove all night and arrived at their vacation cottage early Saturday morning.

9. The game has been postponed because of bad weather and will be rescheduled for later in the season.

10. The sun reflected sharply off the lake and forced me to wear sunglasses.

Review Test 2

Follow the directions given for Review Test 1.

1. The doctors were speaking gently to the parents of the little girl.

2. A rumor has been spreading about the possible closing of the plant.

3. Diesel trucks with heavy exhaust fumes should be banned from the road.

4. The dental assistant should have warned me about the pain.

5. With their fingers, the children started to draw pictures on the steamed window.

6. Three buildings down the street from my house have been demolished.

7. Rats, squirrels, and bats lived in the attic of the abandoned house.

8. Jack and Bob will be anchoring the long-distance team in the track meet.

9. Reluctantly, I crawled from my bed and stumbled to the bathroom.

10. Tiddlywinks, pickup sticks, and hearts were our favorite childhood games.

Subjects and Verbs MASTERY TEST 1

Draw one line under subjects and two lines under verbs. Cross out prepositional phrases as necessary to help find subjects. (Be sure to underline all the parts of a verb. Also, remember that you may find more than one subject and one verb in a sentence.)

1. My son pours chocolate milk on his cereal.

2. A solution to the problem popped suddenly into my head.

3. The salad and potatoes fed only half the guests.

4. That man on the corner may ask you for a quarter.

5. The fallen power line jumped and sparked on the street.

6. Lola likes to walk barefoot across the campus.

7. Nick and Fran sang together and played the piano.

8. The flashing lights of the police car appeared unexpectedly in my rearview mirror.

9. Juan often plays CDs but almost never watches television.

10. We sat by a large rock, munched peanuts, and talked for hours.

NAME: _____

DATE: _____

MASTERY TEST 2 Subjects and Verbs

Draw one line under subjects and two lines under verbs. Cross out prepositional phrases as necessary to help find subjects. (Be sure to underline all the parts of a verb. Also, remember that you may find more than one subject and one verb in a sentence.)

1. I may hitchhike to the Mardi Gras this year.

2. Those tulips make my eyes itch.

3. Layla will be studying all day for the test.

4. Strange behavior in our house is the norm at all hours.

5. The prices of jewelry items in that specialty store have been reduced.

6. Jamon and Yvonne refuse to drive their car at-night.

7. I walked out to the garage last night and ran into a rug on the clothesline.

8. The rising tide will start to wash away that sand castle.

9. Jessica buys clothing impulsively, sends off for lots of mail order items, and in general quickly spends her money.

10. The girls paddled their canoe across the lake and visited some boys at the camp on the other side.

NAME: _____

DATE: _____

Subjects and Verbs

Draw one line under subjects and two lines under verbs. Cross out prepositional phrases as necessary to help find subjects. (Be sure to underline all the parts of a verb. Also, remember that you may find more than one subject and one verb in a sentence.)

1. Olivia believes in extrasensory perception.

2. The drawer of the bureau sticks on rainy days.

3. The little boy squirmed impatiently in his father's arms.

4. The window fan made a clanking sound and kept them awake at night.

5. The shrubs are starting to grow too close to the side of the house.

6. Three members of the basketball team have been suspended from school.

7. Jerry began to study seriously before final exams.

8. The basketball player shouted obscenities at the referee.

9. They won a lifetime supply of dish detergent on the game show but do not have any room for it in their house.

10. The shattered glass, cracked foundations, and fallen signs throughout the city resulted from earthquake tremors.

NAME: _____

DATE: _____

MASTERY TEST 4 # Subjects and Verbs

Draw one line under subjects and two lines under verbs. Cross out prepositional phrases as necessary to help find subjects. (Be sure to underline all the parts of a verb. Also, remember that you may find more than one subject and one verb in a sentence.)

1. The nail under the rug barely missed my toe.

2. I have studied over eight hours for my biology test.

3. Richard and Regina just bought matching sweatshirts.

4. The game has been postponed because of bad weather.

5. Our families played badminton and volleyball at the picnic.

6. Behind all that mud you will see my daughter's face.

7. The beginning of that movie should not be missed.

8. Fred began to exercise seriously after his heart attack.

9. Hakim has been thinking about the job offer but has not made a decision yet.

10. The people on the tour bus dozed, read magazines, talked to each other, or snapped pictures.

Fragments

5

Introductory Activity

Every sentence must have a subject and a verb and must express a complete thought. A word group that lacks a subject or a verb and that does not express a complete thought is a *fragment*.

   Listed below are a number of fragments and sentences. See if you can complete the statement that explains each fragment.

1. Teapots.   *Fragment*

   Teapots whistled.   *Sentence*

   "Teapots" is a fragment because, while it has a subject (*Teapots*), it lacks

   a _____ (*whistled*) and so does not express a complete thought.

2. Instructs.   *Fragment*

   Quincy instructs.   *Sentence*

   "Instructs" is a fragment because, while it has a verb (*Instructs*), it lacks

   a _____ (*Quincy*) and does not express a complete thought.

3. Discussing homework in class.   *Fragment*

   Ellie was discussing homework in class.   *Sentence*

   "Discussing homework in class" is a fragment because it lacks a

   _____ (*Ellie*) and also part of the _____ (*was*). As a result,

   it does not express a complete thought.

continued

4.   When my mother began lecturing me.   *Fragment*

When my mother began lecturing me, I rolled my eyes.   *Sentence*

"When my mother began lecturing me" is a fragment because we want to know *what happened when* the mother began lecturing. The word group does not follow through and express a complete _____.

Answers are on page 559.

What Fragments Are

Every sentence must have a subject and a verb and must express a complete thought. A word group that lacks a subject or a verb and does not express a complete thought is a *fragment*. Following are the most common types of fragments that people write:

1.   Dependent-word fragments
2.   *-ing* and *to* fragments
3.   Added-detail fragments
4.   Missing-subject fragments

Once you understand the specific kind or kinds of fragments that you might write, you should be able to eliminate them from your writing. The following pages explain all four types of fragments.

Dependent-Word Fragments

Some word groups that begin with a dependent word are fragments. Here is a list of common dependent words:

Common Dependent Words

after	unless
although, though	until
as	what, whatever
because	when, whenever
before	where, wherever
even though	whether
how	which, whichever
if, even if	while
in order that	who
since	whose
that, so that	

Whenever you start a sentence with one of these dependent words, you must be careful that a dependent-word fragment does not result. The word group beginning with the dependent word *after* in the selection below is a fragment.

> After I stopped drinking coffee. I began sleeping better at night.

A *dependent statement*—one starting with a dependent word like *after*—cannot stand alone. It depends on another statement to complete the thought. "After I stopped drinking coffee" is a dependent statement. It leaves us hanging. We expect in the same sentence to find out *what happened after* the writer stopped drinking coffee. When a writer does not follow through and complete a thought, a fragment results. To correct the fragment, follow through and complete the thought:

> After I stopped drinking coffee, I began sleeping better at night.

Remember, then, that *dependent statements by themselves* are fragments. They must be attached to a statement that makes sense standing alone.* Here are two other examples of dependent-word fragments.

> Brian sat nervously in the dental clinic. While waiting to have his wisdom tooth pulled.

> Maria decided to throw away the boxes. That had accumulated for years in the basement.

"While waiting to have his wisdom tooth pulled" is a fragment; it does not make sense standing by itself. We want to know in the same statement *what Brian did* while waiting to have his tooth pulled. The writer must complete the thought. Likewise, "That had accumulated for years in the basement" is not in itself a complete thought. We want to know in the same statement what *that* refers to.

How to Correct Dependent-Word Fragments

In most cases, you can correct a dependent-word fragment by attaching it to the sentence that comes after it or to the sentence that comes before it:

> After I stopped drinking coffee, I began sleeping better at night. (The fragment has been attached to the sentence that comes after it.)

> Brian sat nervously in the dental clinic while waiting to have his wisdom tooth pulled. (The fragment has been attached to the sentence that comes before it.)

continued

---

*Some instructors refer to a dependent-word fragment as a *dependent clause*. A *clause* is simply a group of words having a subject and a verb. A clause may be *independent* (expressing a complete thought and able to stand alone) or *dependent* (not expressing a complete thought and not able to stand alone). A dependent clause by itself is a fragment. It can be corrected simply by adding an independent clause.

Maria decided to throw away the boxes that had accumulated for years in the basement. (The fragment has been attached to the sentence that comes before it.)

Another way of correcting a dependent-word fragment is to eliminate the dependent word and make a new sentence:

I stopped drinking coffee.

He was waiting to have his wisdom tooth pulled.

They had accumulated for years in the basement.

Do not use the second method of correction too frequently, however, for it may cut down on interest and variety in your writing style.

TIPS

1. Use a comma if a dependent-word group comes at the *beginning* of a sentence (see also page 357):

After I stopped drinking coffee, I began sleeping better at night.

However, do not generally use a comma if the dependent-word group comes at the end of a sentence:

Brian sat nervously in the dental clinic while waiting to have his wisdom tooth pulled.

Maria decided to throw away the boxes that had accumulated for years in the basement.

2. Sometimes the dependent words *who, that, which,* or *where* appear not at the very start but *near* the start of a word group. A fragment often results.

Today I visited Hilda Cooper. A friend who is in the hospital.

"A friend who is in the hospital" is not in itself a complete thought. We want to know in the same statement *who* the friend is. The fragment can be corrected by attaching it to the sentence that comes before it:

Today I visited Hilda Cooper, a friend who is in the hospital.

(Here a comma is used to set off "a friend who is in the hospital," which is extra material placed at the end of the sentence.)

Practice

1

Turn each of the dependent-word groups into a sentence by adding a complete thought. Put a comma after the dependent-word group if a dependent word starts the sentence.

EXAMPLES

After I got out of high school
After I got out of high school, I spent a year traveling.

The watch that I got fixed
The watch that I got fixed has just stopped working again.

1. After I finished work on Friday

2. Because the class was canceled

3. When my car stalled on the highway

4. The supermarket that I went to

5. Before I left the house

Underline the dependent-word fragment (or fragments) in each item. Then correct each fragment by attaching it to the sentence that comes before or the sentence that comes after—whichever sounds more natural. Put a comma after the dependent-word group if it starts the sentence.

Practice 2

1. Although the air conditioner was working. I still felt warm in the room. I wondered if I had a fever.

2.   When Drew got into his car this morning. He discovered that he had left the car windows open. The seats and rug were soaked. Since it had rained overnight.

_____

_____

_____

3.   After cutting fish at the restaurant all day. Jenny smelled like a cat food factory. She couldn't wait to take a hot, perfumed bath.

_____

_____

_____

4.   Franco raked out the soggy leaves. That were at the bottom of the cement fishpond. When two bullfrogs jumped out at him. He dropped the rake and ran.

_____

_____

_____

5.   Because he had eaten and drunk too much. He had to leave the party early. His stomach was like a volcano. That was ready to erupt.

_____

_____

_____

-ing and to Fragments

When a word ending in -ing or the word to appears at or near the start of a word group, a fragment may result. Such fragments often lack a subject and part of the verb.

Underline the word groups in the examples below that contain -ing words. Each is an -ing fragment.

Example 1

I spent all day in the employment office. Trying to find a job that suited me. The prospects looked bleak.

Example 2

Lola surprised Tony on the nature hike. Picking blobs of resin off pine trees. Then she chewed them like bubble gum.

Example 3

Mel took an aisle seat on the bus. His reason being that he had more legroom.

People sometimes write *-ing* fragments because they think the subject in one sentence will work for the next word group as well. In Example 1, they might think the subject *I* in the opening sentence will also serve as the subject for "Trying to find a job that suited me." But the subject must actually be *in* the sentence.

How to Correct *-ing* Fragments

1. Attach the fragment to the sentence that comes before it or to the sentence that comes after it, whichever makes sense. Example 1 could read, "I spent all day in the employment office, trying to find a job that suited me." (Note that here a comma is used to set off "trying to find a job that suited me," which is extra material placed at the end of the sentence.)

2. Add a subject and change the *-ing* verb part to the correct form of the verb. Example 2 could read, "She picked blobs of resin off pine trees."

3. Change *being* to the correct form of the verb *be (am, are, is, was, were)*. Example 3 could read, "His reason was that he had more legroom."

How to Correct *to* Fragments

As noted on the previous page, when *to* appears at or near the start of a word group, a fragment sometimes results.

> To remind people of their selfishness. Otis leaves handwritten notes on cars that take up two parking spaces.

The first word group in the example above is a *to* fragment. It can be corrected by adding it to the sentence that comes after it.

> To remind people of their selfishness, Otis leaves handwritten notes on cars that take up two parking spaces.

(Note that here a comma is used to set off "To remind people of their selfishness," which is introductory material in the sentence.)

Practice 3

Underline the *-ing* fragment in each of the following selections. Then make the fragment a sentence by rewriting it, using the method described in parentheses.

EXAMPLE

The dog eyed me with suspicion. <u>Not knowing whether its master was at home.</u> I hesitated to open the gate.

(Add the fragment to the sentence that comes after it.)

Not knowing whether its master was at home, I hesitated to open the gate.

_____

1. Eli lay in bed after the alarm rang. Wishing that he had one million dollars. Then he would not have to go to work.
   (Add the fragment to the preceding sentence.)

   _____

   _____

2. Investigating the strange, mournful cries in his neighbor's yard. George found a puppy tangled in its leash.
   (Add the fragment to the sentence that comes after it.)

   _____

   _____

3. I had to drive to the most remote parking lot to get a space. As a result, being late for class.
   (Add the subject *I* and change *being* to the correct form of the verb *was*.)

   _____

   _____

Practice 4

Underline the *-ing* or *to* fragment in each item. Then rewrite the item correctly, using one of the methods of correction described on page 85.

1. Glistening with dew. The gigantic web hung between the branches of the tree. The spider waited patiently for a visitor.

   _____

   _____

   _____

2. Kevin loves his new puppy. Claiming that the little dog is his best friend.

   _____

   _____

3. Noah picked through the box of chocolates. Removing the kinds he didn't like. He saved these for his wife and ate the rest.

    _____

    _____

4. The grass I was walking on suddenly became squishy. Having hiked into a marsh of some kind.

    _____

    _____

    _____

5. Steve drove quickly to the bank. To cash his paycheck. Otherwise, he would have had no money for the weekend.

    _____

    _____

    _____

Added-Detail Fragments

Added-detail fragments lack a subject and a verb. They often begin with one of the following words or phrases.

also	except	including
especially	for example	such as

See if you can underline the one added-detail fragment in each of these examples:

Example 1

Tony has trouble accepting criticism. Except from Lola. She has a knack for tact.

Example 2

My apartment has its drawbacks. For example, no hot water in the morning.

Example 3

I had many jobs while in school. Among them, busboy, painter, and security guard.

People often write added-detail fragments for much the same reason they write *-ing* fragments. They think the subject and verb in one sentence will serve for the next word group as well. But the subject and verb must be in *each* word group.

> **How to** Correct Added-Detail Fragments
>
> 1. Attach the fragment to the complete thought that precedes it. Example 1 could read, "Tony has trouble accepting criticism, except from Lola." (Note that here a comma is used to set off "except from Lola," which is extra material placed at the end of the sentence.)
>
> 2. Add a subject and a verb to the fragment to make it a complete sentence. Example 2 could read, "My apartment has its drawbacks. For example, there is no hot water in the morning."
>
> 3. Change words as necessary to make the fragment part of the preceding sentence. Example 3 could read, "Among the many jobs I had while in school were busboy, painter, and security guard."

Practice

5

Underline the fragment in each selection below. Then make it a sentence by rewriting it, using the method described in parentheses.

EXAMPLE

My husband and I share the household chores. <u>Including meals.</u> I do the cooking and he does the eating.
(Add the fragment to the preceding sentence.)

My husband and I share the household chores, including meals.

1. Hakeem is very accident-prone. For example, managing to cut his hand while crumbling a bar of shredded wheat.
   (Correct the fragment by adding the subject *he* and changing *managing* to *managed.*)

   _____

   _____

2. Tina's job in the customer service department depressed her. All day, people complained. About missing parts, rude salespeople, and errors on bills.
   (Add the fragment to the preceding sentence.)

   _____

   _____

3. My mother is always giving me household hints. For example, using club
   soda on stains. Unfortunately, I never remember them.
   (Correct the fragment by adding the subject and verb *she suggests.*)

_____

_____

Underline the added-detail fragment in each selection. Then rewrite that part of
the selection needed to correct the fragment. Use one of the three methods of correction described on page 88.

Practice

6

1. My little boy is constantly into mischief. Such as tearing the labels off all
   the cans in the cupboard.

_____

_____

2. The old house was filled with expensive woodwork. For example, a hand-
   carved mantel and a mahogany banister.

_____

_____

3. Andy used to have many bad eating habits. For instance, chewing with his
   mouth open.

_____

_____

4. I put potatoes in the oven without first punching holes in them. A half hour
   later, there were several explosions. With potatoes splattering all over the
   walls of the oven.

_____

_____

5. Janet looked forward to seeing former classmates at the high school reunion.
   Including the football player she had had a wild crush on. She wondered if
   he had grown fat and bald.

_____

_____

Missing-Subject Fragments

In each example below, underline the word group in which the subject is missing.

Example 1

One example of my father's generosity is that he visits sick friends in the hospital. And takes along get-well cards with a few dollars folded in them.

Example 2

The weight lifter grunted as he heaved the barbells into the air. Then, with a loud groan, dropped them.

People write missing-subject fragments because they think the subject in one sentence will apply to the next word group as well. But the subject, as well as the verb, must be in *each* word group to make it a sentence.

How to	Correct Missing-Subject Fragments

1. Attach the fragment to the preceding sentence. Example 1 could read, "One illustration of my father's generosity is that he visits sick friends in the hospital and takes along get-well cards with a few dollars folded in them."

2. Add a subject (which can often be a pronoun standing for the subject in the preceding sentence). Example 2 could read, "Then, with a loud groan, he dropped them."

Practice

7

Underline the missing-subject fragment in each selection. Then rewrite that part of the selection needed to correct the fragment. Use one of the two methods of correction described above.

1. Fred went to the refrigerator to get milk for his breakfast cereal. And discovered about one tablespoon of milk left in the carton.

_____

_____

2. At the laundromat, I loaded the dryer with wet clothes. Then noticed the "Out of Order" sign taped over the coin slot.

_____

_____

3. Our neighborhood's most eligible bachelor got married this weekend. But did not invite us to the wedding. We all wondered what the bride was like.

    _____

    _____

4. Larry's father could not accept his son's lifestyle. Also, was constantly criticizing Larry's choice of friends.

    _____

    _____

5. Wanda stared at the blank page in desperation. And decided that the first sentence of a paper is always the hardest to write.

    _____

    _____

A REVIEW

How to Check for Fragments

www.mhhe.com/langan

1. Read your paper aloud from the *last* sentence to the *first*. You will be better able to see and hear whether each word group you read is a complete thought.

2. If you think any word group is a fragment, ask yourself, Does this contain a subject and a verb and express a complete thought?

3. More specifically, be on the lookout for the most common fragments.

    • Dependent-word fragments (starting with words like *after, because, since, when,* and *before*)

    • *-ing* and *to* fragments (*-ing* or *to* at or near the start of a word group)

    • Added-detail fragments (starting with words like *for example, such as, also,* and *especially*)

    • Missing-subject fragments (a verb is present but not the subject)

Collaborative Activity

Editing and Rewriting

Working with a partner, read the short paragraph below and underline the five fragments. Then correct the fragments. Feel free to discuss the rewrite quietly with your partner and refer back to the chapter when necessary.

¹I am only thirty, but a trip to the movies recently made me realize that my youth is definitely past. ²The science-fiction movie had attracted a large audience of younger kids and teenagers. ³Before the movie began. ⁴Groups of kids ran up and down the aisles, laughing, giggling, and spilling popcorn. ⁵I was annoyed with them. ⁶But thought, "At one time I was doing the same thing. ⁷Now I'm acting like one of the adults." ⁸The thought was a little depressing, for I remembered how much fun it was not to care what the adults thought. ⁹Soon after the movie began, a group of teenagers walked in and sat in the first row. ¹⁰During the movie, they vied with each other. ¹¹To see who could make the loudest comment. ¹²Or the most embarrassing noise. ¹³Some of the adults in the theater complained to the usher, but I had a guilty memory about doing the same thing myself a few times. ¹⁴In addition, a teenage couple was sitting in front of me. ¹⁵Occasionally, these two held hands or the boy put his arm around the girl. ¹⁶A few times, they sneaked a kiss. ¹⁷Realizing that my wife and I were long past this kind of behavior in the movies. ¹⁸I again felt like an old man.

Collaborative Activity

Creating Sentences

Working with a partner, make up your own short fragments test as directed. Write one or more of your sentences about the photo shown here.

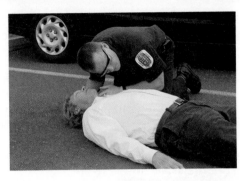

1. Write a dependent-word fragment in the space below. Then correct the fragment by making it into a complete sentence. You may want to begin your fragment with the word *before, after, when, because,* or *if.*

    Fragment _____

    Sentence _____

    _____

2. Write a fragment that begins with a word that has an *-ing* ending in the space below. Then correct the fragment by making it into a complete sentence. You may want to begin your fragment with the word *laughing, walking, shopping,* or *talking.*

    Fragment _____

    Sentence _____

    _____

3. Write an added-detail fragment in the space below. Then correct the fragment by making it into a complete sentence. You may want to begin your fragment with the word *also, especially, except,* or *including.*

    Fragment _____

    Sentence _____

    _____

Reflective Activity

1. Look at the paragraph about going to the movies that you revised. How has removing fragments affected the reading of the paragraph? Explain.

2. Explain what it is about fragments that you find most difficult to remember and apply. Use an example to make your point clear. Feel free to refer to anything in this chapter.

Review Test 1

Turn each of the following word groups into a complete sentence. Use the space provided.

EXAMPLES

Feeling very confident

Feeling very confident, I began my speech.

Until the rain started

We played softball until the rain started.

1. Before you sit down

_____

2. When the noise stopped

_____

3. To get to the game on time

_____

4. During my walk along the trail

_____

5. Because I was short on cash

_____

6. Lucy, whom I know well

_____

NAME: _____

DATE: _____

SCORE
Number Correct

_____ x 10

_____ %

Underline the fragment in each item. Then make whatever changes are needed to turn the fragment into a sentence.

EXAMPLE

In grade school, I didn't want to wear glasses. And avoided having to get them by memorizing the Snellen eye chart.

1. I rang their doorbell for ten minutes. Finally deciding no one was home. I stalked away in disgust.

2. According to the latest weather report. Heavy rains will fall for the next twenty-four hours. Flash floods are expected.

3. A ceiling should be painted a very light color. Such as white or pale beige. Then the room will seem larger.

4. My classes all being in the afternoon this semester. I can sleep until noon every day. My roommate hates me for it.

5. The plumber told us he could fix the leak in our shower. But would not be able to come until next month.

6. I spent an hour in the mall parking lot yesterday. Looking for my gray compact car. There were hundreds of other cars just like it in the lot.

7. Tony filled in the three-page application. Then he waited to see the personnel manager. Who would interview him for the position.

8. Suddenly the pitcher turned around. And threw to first base. But the runn already standing on second.

9. Staggering under the weight of the heavy laundry basket. N⁹ down the basement steps. Then he discovered the washer wa'

10. My brother spends a lot of time at the mall. There is an Space Port. Where he meets his friends and plays video gan.

NAME: _____

DATE: _____

MASTERY TEST 3 | # Fragments

Underline the fragment in each item. Then make whatever changes are needed to turn the fragment into a sentence.

1. Susie turned in her exam book. Then she walked out of the room. Wondering if she had passed.

2. The manager was fined $10,000. He had knocked the umpire's cap off his head. And kicked it across the infield.

3. Lola's printer was giving her trouble. All the y's were losing their tails. And looked like v's.

4. My little brother enjoys playing practical jokes. On anyone who visits our house. He even tells people that our house is haunted.

5. Because she had not studied for the exam. Susie was very nervous. If she got a passing grade, it would be a miracle.

6. Customers were lined up ten-deep at every entrance. Waiting for the store to open. Everything was on sale at 50 percent off.

7. Eva often gets up very early. Sometimes as early as 6 A.M. She says she thinks most clearly in the mornings.

8. We loaded the car with camping gear. Including a four-burner Coleman stove and a portable television.

9. James has a terrible problem. Unless he can scrape together three hundred dollars for his monthly installment. He will lose his new Honda.

10. The unusual meeting began at 3 P.M. But adjourned at 3:05 P.M. Nobody could think of anything to talk about.

Fragments MASTERY TEST 4

Underline and then correct the ten fragments in the following passage.

When my mother was a young girl. She spent several summers on her aunt and uncle's farm. To this day she has vivid memories of the chores she did on the farm. Such as shucking corn for dinners and for canning. As she pulled off the moist brown cornsilk. Yellow worms would wiggle on the ear or drop off into her lap. Another task was preparing string beans. Which had to be picked over before the beans would be cooked. My mother and her aunt spent hours snapping the ends off the beans. And tossing each one into a large basin. But the chore my mother remembers most clearly is preparing a chicken for Sunday dinner. Her aunt would head for the chicken yard. Somehow, the chickens seemed to know her purpose. They ran wildly in all directions. Fluttering and squawking, or fleeing into the henhouse. When Aunt Helen found the right chicken. She picked it up and gave its neck a quick twist. Killing it instantly. Back in the kitchen, she and my mother would gut the chicken. And pluck its feathers out, down to the last tiny pinfeather. One special treat came out of this bloody chore. My mother always got the chicken feet to play with. Their long white tendons still attached. As my mother pulled on the tendons, the claws opened and closed like mechanical toys. My mother loved to terrorize her friends with these moving claws.

NAME: _____

DATE: _____

MASTERY TEST 5 | # Fragments

The passage that follows contains five fragments. Underline the fragments and then correct them in the space provided.

[1]If you have ever gone to a casino, club, or a neighborhood bar. [2]You probably have inhaled secondhand smoke. [3]In most states, nonsmokers must tolerate smoke in public places. [4]Treating it as if it were just a smelly annoyance. [5]However, research proves that secondhand smoke is linked to serious health problems. [6]One study shows that nonsmokers who live with smokers have a 30 percent greater chance of getting lung cancer. [7]And are at a higher risk for heart disease. [8]Children who live with smokers have increased chances of life-threatening medical conditions. [9]Including lung infections, severe asthma, and sudden infant death syndrome. [10]Even those who don't live with smokers can be harmed by brief exposures to secondhand smoke, which quickly affects the arteries and threatens people at high risk of heart disease. [11]To date, only fifteen states have comprehensive laws. [12]That protect people from secondhand smoke.

1. _____

_____

2. _____

_____

3. _____

_____

4. _____

_____

5. _____

_____

Run-Ons

6

Introductory Activity

A run-on occurs when two sentences are run together with no adequate sign given to mark the break between them. Shown below are four run-on sentences and four correctly marked sentences. See if you can complete the statement that explains how each run-on is corrected.

1. A student yawned in class the result was a chain reaction of copycat yawning.

    A student yawned in class. The result was a chain reaction of copycat yawning.

The run-on has been corrected by using a _____ and a capital letter to separate the two complete thoughts.

2. I placed an ad in the paper last week, no one has replied.

    I placed an ad in the paper last week, but no one has replied.

The run-on has been corrected by using a joining word, _____, to connect the two complete thoughts.

3. A bus barreled down the street, it splashed murky rainwater all over the pedestrians.

    A bus barreled down the street; it splashed murky rainwater all over the pedestrians.

continued

The run-on has been corrected by using a _____ to connect the two closely related thoughts.

4.   I had a campus map, I still could not find my classroom building.

Although I had a campus map, I still could not find my classroom building.

The run-on has been corrected by using the dependent word _____ to connect the two closely related thoughts.

Answers are on page 560.

What Are Run-Ons?

www.mhhe.com/langan

A *run-on* is two complete thoughts that are run together with no adequate sign given to mark the break between them. As a result of the run-on, the reader is confused, unsure of where one thought ends and the next one begins. Two types of run-ons are fused sentences and comma splices.

Some run-ons have no punctuation at all to mark the break between the thoughts. Such run-ons are known as *fused sentences:* they are fused or joined together as if they were only one thought.

Fused Sentence

Rosa decided to stop smoking she didn't want to die of lung cancer.

Fused Sentence

The exam was postponed the class was canceled as well.

In other run-ons, known as *comma splices,* a comma is used to connect or "splice" together the two complete thoughts.* However, a comma alone is *not enough* to connect two complete thoughts. Some connection stronger than a comma alone is needed.

---

*Notes:
1. Some instructors feel that the term *run-ons* should be applied only to fused sentences, not to comma splices. But for many other instructors, and for our purposes in this book, the term *run-on* applies equally to fused sentences and comma splices. The bottom line is that you do not want either fused sentences or comma splices in your writing.
2. Some instructors refer to each complete thought in a run-on as an *independent clause.* A *clause* is simply a group of words having a subject and a verb. A clause may be *independent* (expressing a complete thought and able to stand alone) or *dependent* (not expressing a complete thought and not able to stand alone). A run-on is two independent clauses that are run together with no adequate sign given to mark the break between them.

Comma Splice

Rosa decided to stop smoking, she didn't want to die of lung cancer.

Comma Splice

The exam was postponed, the class was canceled as well.

Comma splices are the most common kind of run-on. Students sense that some kind of connection is needed between thoughts, and so they put a comma at the dividing point. But the comma alone is *not sufficient.* A stronger, clearer mark is needed between the two thoughts.

A Warning: Words That Can Lead to Run-Ons

People often write run-ons when the second complete thought begins with one of the following words:

I	**we**	**there**	**now**
you	**they**	**this**	**then**
he, she, it		**that**	**next**

Remember to be on the alert for run-ons whenever you use these words in your writing.

Correcting Run-Ons

Here are four common methods of correcting a run-on:

1. Use a period and a capital letter to separate the two complete thoughts. (In other words, make two separate sentences of the two complete thoughts.)

   Rosa decided to stop smoking. She didn't want to die of lung cancer.

   The exam was postponed. The class was canceled as well.

2. Use a comma plus a joining word (*and, but, for, or, nor, so, yet*) to connect the two complete thoughts.

   Rosa decided to stop smoking, for she didn't want to die of lung cancer.

   The exam was postponed, and the class was canceled as well.

3. Use a semicolon to connect the two complete thoughts.

   Rosa decided to stop smoking; she didn't want to die of lung cancer.

   The exam was postponed; the class was canceled as well.

continued

> 4. Use subordination (put a dependent word at the beginning of one fragment).
>
> Because Rosa didn't want to die of lung cancer, she decided to stop smoking.
>
> When the exam was postponed, the class was canceled as well.

The following pages will give you practice in all four methods of correcting run-ons. The use of subordination will be explained further on page 133, in a chapter that deals with sentence variety.

Method 1: Period and a Capital Letter

One way of correcting a run-on is to use a period and a capital letter at the break between the two complete thoughts. Use this method especially if the thoughts are not closely related or if another method would make the sentence too long.

Practice

1

Locate the split in each of the following run-ons. Each is a *fused sentence*—that is, each consists of two sentences fused or joined together with no punctuation at all between them. Reading each sentence aloud will help you "hear" where a major break or split in the thought occurs. At such a point, your voice will probably drop and pause.

Correct the run-on by putting a period at the end of the first thought and a capital letter at the start of the second thought.

EXAMPLE

Gary was not a success at his job. *H* his mouth moved faster than his hands.

1. Gerald's motorized wheelchair broke down he was unable to go to class.

2. The subway train hurtled through the station a blur of spray paint and graffiti flashed in front of my eyes.

3. Jenny panicked the car had stalled on a treacherous traffic circle.

4. Half the class flunked the exam the other half of the students were absent.

5. One reason for the high cost of new furniture is the cost of good wood one walnut tree sold recently for $40,000.

6. The wedding reception began to get out of hand guests started to throw cake at each other.

7. Jamal's pitchfork turned over the rich earth earthworms poked their heads out of new furrows.

8. There were a lot of unusual people at the party a few of the women had shaved heads.

9. Carol talks all the time her tongue is getting calluses.

10. Hundreds of crushed cars were piled in neat stacks the rusted hulks resembled flattened tin cans.

Locate the split in each of the following run-ons. Some of the run-ons are fused sentences, and some of them are *comma splices*—run-ons spliced or joined together only with a comma. Correct each run-on by putting a period at the end of the first thought and a capital letter at the start of the next thought.

Practice 2

1. I wish Carl wouldn't fall asleep in class, his snoring drowns out the lecture.

2. The crime rate in this country is increasing, every eight seconds another home is burglarized.

3. Our car radio is not working properly we get whistling noises and static instead of music.

4. That shopping mall has the smell of death about it half the stores are empty.

5. Cats sleep in all sorts of unusual places, our new cat likes to curl up in the bathroom sink.

6. Every day, Americans use 450 billion gallons of water this amount would cover New York City to a depth of 96 feet.

7. The driver had an unusual excuse for speeding, he said he had just washed his car and was trying to dry it.

8. The telephone rang at least fifteen times, nobody felt like getting up to answer it.

9. Some of our foods have misleading names, for example, English muffins were actually invented in America.

10. The soccer star raised his arms in victory his shot sailed into the goal.

Write a second sentence to go with each sentence below. Start the second sentence with the word given in the margin.

Practice 3

EXAMPLE

He   My dog's ears snapped up. *He had heard a wolf howling on television.*

They   1. I could not find my car keys. _____

_____

Then   2. The first thing Marcus ate for dessert was a peach. _____

_____

She   3. My daughter began screaming. _____

_____

It   4. The toaster oven was acting strangely. _____

_____

There   5. Cars had to stop suddenly at the intersection. _____

_____

Method 2: Comma and a Joining Word

Another way of correcting a run-on is to use a comma plus a joining word to connect the two complete thoughts. Joining words (also called *coordinating conjunctions*) include *and, but, for, or, nor, so,* and *yet.* Here is what the four most common joining words mean:

and   in addition, along with

Natalie was watching Monday night football, and she was doing her homework as well.

(*And* means *in addition:* Natalie was watching Monday night football; *in addition,* she was doing her homework.)

but   however, except, on the other hand, just the opposite

I voted for the president two years ago, but I would not vote for him today.

(*But* means *however:* I voted for the president two years ago; *however,* I would not vote for him today.)

for   because, the reason why, the cause for something

Saturday is the worst day to shop, for people jam the stores.

(*For* means *because:* Saturday is the worst day to shop *because* people jam the stores.) If you are not comfortable using *for,* you may want to use *because* instead of *for* in the activities that follow. If you do use *because,* omit the comma before it.

SO   as a result, therefore

Our son misbehaved again, so he was sent upstairs without dessert.

(*So* means *as a result:* Our son misbehaved again; *as a result,* he was sent upstairs without dessert.)

Insert the comma and the joining word (*and, but, for, so*) that logically connects the two thoughts in each sentence.

Practice

4

EXAMPLE

A trip to the zoo always depresses me, *for* I hate to see animals in cages.

1. The telephone was ringing someone was at the front door as well.

2. Something was obviously wrong with the meat loaf it was glowing in the dark.

3. Tia and Nina enjoyed the movie they wished the seats had been more comfortable.

4. Brett moved from Boston to Los Angeles he wanted to get as far away as possible from his ex-wife.

5. I decided to go back to school I felt my brain was turning to slush.

6. Lola loved the rose cashmere sweater she had nothing to wear with it.

7. Art's son has joined the Army his daughter is thinking of joining, too.

8. Lydia began working the second shift she is not able to eat supper with her family anymore.

9. Fred remembered to get the hamburger he forgot to buy the hamburger rolls.

10. My TV wasn't working I walked over to a friend's house to watch the game.

Practice

5

Add a complete, closely related thought to each of the following statements. When you write the second thought, use a comma plus the joining word shown at the left.

EXAMPLE

but   I was sick with the flu, _____*but I still had to study for the test.*_____

so   1. The night was hot and humid _____

_____

but   2. Fred wanted to get a pizza _____

_____

and   3. Lola went shopping in the morning _____

_____

for   4. I'm going to sell my car _____

_____

but   5. I expected the exam to be easy _____

_____

Method 3: Semicolon

A third method of correcting a run-on is to use a semicolon to mark the break between two thoughts. A *semicolon* (;) is made up of a period above a comma and is sometimes called a *strong comma.* The semicolon signals more of a pause than a comma alone but not quite the full pause of a period.

Occasional use of semicolons can add variety to sentences. For some people, however, the semicolon is a confusing mark of punctuation. Keep in mind that if you are not comfortable using it, you can and should use one of the first two methods of correcting a run-on sentence.

Semicolon Alone

Here are some earlier sentences that were connected with a comma plus a joining word. Now they are connected with a semicolon. Notice that a semicolon, unlike a comma, can be used alone to connect the two complete thoughts in each sentence.

Natalie was watching Monday night football; she was doing her homework as well.

I voted for the president two years ago; I would not vote for him today.

Saturday is the worst day to shop; people jam the stores.

Insert a semicolon where the break occurs between the two complete thoughts in each of the following sentences.

EXAMPLE

She had a wig on; it looked more like a hat than a wig.

1. I just canceled my cell phone service the bill was just too expensive.

2. Reggie wanted to watch *American Idol* the rest of the family insisted on watching a movie.

3. Bonnie put a freshly baked batch of chocolate chip cookies on the counter to cool everyone gathered round for samples.

4. About $25 million worth of pizza is eaten each year an average of three hundred new pizza parlors open every week.

5. Nate never heard the third base coach screaming for him to stop he was out at home plate by ten feet.

Semicolon with a Transition

A semicolon is sometimes used with a transitional word and a comma to join two complete thoughts:

I figured that the ball game would cost me about ten dollars; however, I didn't consider the high price of food and drinks.

Fred and Martha have a low-interest mortgage on their house; otherwise, they would move to another neighborhood.

Sharon didn't understand the instructor's point; therefore, she asked him to repeat it.

TIP Sometimes transitional words do not join complete thoughts but are merely interrupters in a sentence (see pages 358–359):

My parents, moreover, plan to go on the trip.
I believe, however, that they'll change their minds.

Transitional Words

Here is a list of common transitional words (also called *adverbial conjunctions*).

Common Transitional Words		
however	moreover	therefore
on the other hand	in addition	as a result
nevertheless	also	consequently
instead	furthermore	otherwise

Practice

7

For each item, choose a logical transitional word from the box above and write it in the space provided. In addition, put a semicolon *before* the transition and a comma *after* it.

EXAMPLE

It was raining harder than ever _; however,_ Bobby was determined to go to the amusement park.

1. The tree must be sprayed with insecticide _____ the spider mites will kill it.

2. I helped the magician set up his props _____ I agreed to let him saw me in half.

3. Fred never finished paneling his basement _____ he hired a carpenter to complete the job.

4. My house was robbed last week _____ I bought a watchdog.

5. Juanita is taking five courses this semester _____ she is working forty hours a week.

Practice

8

Punctuate each sentence by using a semicolon and a comma.

EXAMPLE

Our tap water has a funny taste;consequently,we buy bottled water to drink.

1. I arrived early to get a good seat however there were already a hundred people outside the door.

2. Foul language marred the live boxing match as a result next time the network will probably use a tape delay.

3. The fluorescent lights in the library gave Jan a headache furthermore they distracted her by making a loud humming sound.

4. The broken shells on the beach were like tiny razors consequently we walked along with extreme caution.

5. Ted carefully combed and recombed his hair nevertheless his bald spot still showed.

Method 4: Subordination

A fourth method of joining related thoughts is to use subordination. *Subordination* is a way of showing that one thought in a sentence is not as important as another thought. Here are three sentences in which one idea is subordinated to (made less emphatic than) the other idea:

Because Rosa didn't want to die of lung cancer, she decided to stop smoking.

The wedding reception began to get out of hand when the guests started to throw food at each other.

Although my brothers wanted to watch a *Star Trek* rerun, the rest of the family insisted on turning to the network news.

Dependent Words

Notice that when we subordinate, we use dependent words like *because, when,* and *although.* Following is a brief list of common dependent words (see the complete list on page 128). Subordination is explained in full on pages 133–134.

Common Dependent Words		
after	before	unless
although	even though	until
as	if	when
because	since	while

Choose a logical dependent word from the box above and write it in the space provided.

EXAMPLE

Although going up a ladder is easy, looking down can be difficult.

1. The instructor is lowering my grade in the course _____ I was late for class three times.

2. _____ the airplane dropped a few feet, my stomach rose a few feet.

3. _____ the football game was being played, we sent out for a pizza.

4. _____ the football game was over, we went out for another pizza.

5. You should talk to a counselor _____ you decide on your courses for next semester.

Practice

9

Rewrite the five sentences below, taken from this chapter, so that one idea is subordinate to the other. In each case, use one of the dependent words in the box on page 113.

EXAMPLE

My house was burglarized last week; I bought a watchdog.

Because my house was burglarized last week, I bought a watchdog.

> **HINT** As in the example, use a comma if a dependent statement starts a sentence.

1. Sharon didn't understand the instructor's point; she asked him to repeat it.

   _____

   _____

2. Marco remembered to get the hamburger; he forgot to get the hamburger rolls.

   _____

   _____

3. Michael gulped two cups of strong coffee; his heart started to flutter.

   _____

   _____

4. A car sped around the corner; it sprayed slush all over the pedestrians.

   _____

   _____

5. Lola loved the rose cashmere sweater; she had nothing to wear with it.

   _____

   _____

Collaborative Activity

Editing and Rewriting

Working with a partner, read carefully the short paragraph below and underline the five run-ons. Then use the space provided to correct the five run-ons. Feel free to discuss the rewrite quietly with your partner and refer back to the chapter when necessary.

[1]When Mark began his first full-time job, he immediately got a credit card, a used sports car was his first purchase. [2]Then he began to buy expensive clothes that he could not afford he also bought impressive gifts for his parents and his girlfriend. [3]Several months passed before Mark realized that he owed an enormous amount of money. [4]To make matters worse, his car broke down, a stack of bills suddenly seemed to be due at once. [5]Mark tried to cut back on his purchases, he soon realized he had to cut up his credit card to prevent himself from using it. [6]He also began keeping a careful record of his spending he had no idea where his money had gone till then. [7]He hated to admit to his family and friends that he had to get his budget under control. [8]However, his girlfriend said she did not mind inexpensive dates, and his parents were proud of his growing maturity.

_____

_____

_____

_____

_____

_____

_____

_____

Collaborative Activity

Creating Sentences

Working with a partner, make up your own short run-ons test as directed.

1. Write a run-on sentence. Then rewrite it, using a period and capital letter to separate the thoughts into two sentences.

    Run-on _____

    _____

    Rewrite _____

    _____

2. Write a sentence that has two complete thoughts. Then rewrite it, using a comma and a joining word to correctly join the complete thoughts.

    Two complete thoughts _____

    _____

    Rewrite _____

    _____

3. Write a sentence that has two complete thoughts. Then rewrite it, using a semicolon to correctly join the complete thoughts.

    Two complete thoughts _____

    _____

    Rewrite _____

    _____

Reflective Activity

1. Look at the paragraph about Mark that you revised above. Explain how run-ons interfere with your reading of the paragraph.

2. In your own written work, which type of run-on are you most likely to write: comma splices or fused sentences? Why do you tend to make the kind of mistake that you do?

3. Which method for correcting run-ons are you most likely to use in your own writing? Which are you least likely to use? Why?

Review Test 1

Some of the run-ons that follow are *fused sentences,* having no punctuation between the two complete thoughts; others are *comma splices,* having only a comma between the two complete thoughts.

Correct the run-ons by using one of the following three methods:

- Period and a capital letter
- Comma and a joining word (*and, but, for, so*)
- Semicolon

Use whichever method seems most appropriate in each case.

EXAMPLE

Fred pulled the cellophane off the cake, the icing came along with it.

1. I found the cat sleeping on the stove the dog was eating the morning mail.

2. Yoko has a twenty-mile drive to school she sometimes arrives late for class.

3. I lifted the empty water bottle above me a few more drops fell out of it and into my thirsty mouth.

4. These pants are guaranteed to wear like iron they also feel like iron.

5. I saw a black-and-white blob on the highway soon the odor of skunk wafted through my car.

6. She gets A's in her math homework by using her pocket calculator she is not allowed to use the calculator at school.

7. Flies were getting into the house the window screen was torn.

8. Martha moans and groans upon getting up in the morning she sounds like a crazy woman.

9. Lola met Tony at McDonald's they shared a large order of fries.

10. The carpet in their house needs to be replaced the walls should be painted as well.

Review Test 2

Correct the run-on in each sentence by using subordination. Choose from among the following dependent words.

after	before	unless
although	even though	until
as	if	when
because	since	while

EXAMPLE

Tony hated going to a new barber, he was afraid his hair would be butchered.

Because Tony was afraid his hair would be butchered, he hated going to a new

barber.

1. The meal and conversation were enjoyable, I kept worrying about the check.

2. My wet fingers stuck to the frosty ice cube tray, I had to pry them loose.

3. I take a late afternoon nap, my mind and body are refreshed and ready for my night course.

4. Our daughter jumped up screaming a black spider was on her leg.

5. I wanted badly to cry I remained cold and silent.

6. Lisa does the food shopping every two weeks she first cashes her paycheck at the bank.

_____

_____

7. Follow the instructions carefully, you'll have the computer set up and working in no time.

_____

_____

8. Every child in the neighborhood was in the backyard, Frank stepped outside to investigate.

_____

_____

9. My first year in college was not a success, I spent most of my time in the game room.

_____

_____

10. A burglar was in our upstairs bedroom going through our drawers, we were in the den downstairs watching television.

_____

_____

Review Test   3

On separate paper, write six sentences, each of which has two complete thoughts. In two of the sentences, use a period and a capital letter between the thoughts. In another two sentences, use a comma and a joining word (*and, but, or, nor, for, so, yet*) to join the thoughts. In the final two sentences, use a semicolon to join the thoughts.

Review Test   4

Write for five minutes about something that makes you angry. Don't worry about spelling, punctuation, finding exact words, or organizing your thoughts. Just focus on writing as many words as you can without stopping.

After you have finished, go back and make whatever changes are needed to correct any run-on sentences in your writing.

MASTERY TEST 1 | Run-Ons

In the space provided, write *R-O* beside run-on sentences. Write *C* beside the one sentence that is punctuated correctly. Some of the run-ons have no punctuation between the two complete thoughts; others have only a comma.

Correct each run-on by using (1) a period and a capital letter, (2) a comma and a joining word, or (3) a semicolon. Do not use the same method of correction for every sentence.

EXAMPLES

___*R-O*___   I applied for the job, ^{but} I never got called in for an interview.

___*R-O*___   Carla's toothache is getting worse; she should go to a dentist soon.

_____   1. I had a very bad headache I felt light-headed and feverish as well.

_____   2. Our children have the newest electronic games the house sounds like a video arcade.

_____   3. Two men held up the ski shop, they were wearing masks.

_____   4. Swirls of dust flew across the field good topsoil vanished into the distance.

_____   5. I cannot get a definite commitment from Beth I decided not to count on her.

_____   6. The soup was too hot to eat, so I dropped in two ice cubes and cooled it off quickly.

_____   7. The course on the history of UFOs sounded interesting it turned out to be very dull.

_____   8. That clothing store is a strange place to visit, you keep walking up to dummies that look like real people.

_____   9. Luisa throws out old pieces of soap, for she can't stand the sharp edges of the worn-down bars.

_____   10. The oil warning light came on Gerry foolishly continued to drive the car.

NAME: _____

DATE: _____

Run-Ons MASTERY TEST 2

In the space provided, write *R-O* beside run-on sentences. Write *C* beside the two sentences that are punctuated correctly. Some of the run-ons have no punctuation between the two complete thoughts; others have only a comma.

Correct each run-on by using (1) a period and a capital letter, (2) a comma and a joining word, or (3) a semicolon. Do not use the same method of correction for every sentence.

_____ 1. This semester Melissa has three different jobs she barely has enough time to sleep.

_____ 2. First Nick grilled three hamburgers, and then he placed a slice of cheese on each one.

_____ 3. Cats make ideal pets they are clean and require less attention than other animals.

_____ 4. Kathy is afraid of snakes she trembles in fear at the thought of seeing one.

_____ 5. I began to get sleepy during the long drive home, so I pulled over and took a short nap.

_____ 6. The batter hit the baseball it rocketed over the fence for a game-winning home run.

_____ 7. The average person needs at least eight hours of sleep each night most people get less than seven hours of sleep nightly.

_____ 8. Residents rejected a plan to build a stadium in their community they feared major traffic problems.

_____ 9. I spoke to the police officer in a friendly tone I hoped to avoid getting a speeding ticket.

_____ 10. Our landlord raised our rent twice in one year we are now looking for a new place to live.

NAME: _____

DATE: _____

MASTERY TEST 3 ## Run-Ons

In the space provided, write *R-O* beside run-on sentences. Write *C* beside the two sentences that are punctuated correctly. Some of the run-ons have no punctuation between the two complete thoughts; others have only a comma.

Correct each run-on by using (1) a period and capital letter, (2) a comma and a joining word, or (3) a semicolon. Do not use the same method of correction for every sentence.

_____ 1. Shayla does yoga exercises every morning she strongly believes in a healthy body.

_____ 2. Fast cars and fast people can be lots of fun, but they can also be very dangerous.

_____ 3. I wondered why the time was passing so slowly then I realized my watch had stopped.

_____ 4. Bill can crush walnuts with his teeth he is also good at biting the caps off of beer bottles.

_____ 5. At one time Bill used to bend nails with his teeth this practice ended when a wise guy slipped him a hardened nail.

_____ 6. My dentist teaches part-time in a neighborhood clinic he refers to himself as a drill instructor.

_____ 7. An improperly placed goldfish bowl can start a house fire, sunlight reflects and magnifies through the bowl glass.

_____ 8. At the crack of dawn, our neighbors start up their lawn mowers, and the Saturday morning symphony begins.

_____ 9. Kevin had a bad headache yesterday, moreover, his arthritis was bothering him.

_____ 10. As a little girl, she pretended she was a hairdresser her closet was full of bald dolls.

Run-Ons MASTERY TEST 4

In the space provided, write *R-O* beside run-on sentences. Write *C* beside the one sentence that is punctuated correctly. Some of the run-ons have no punctuation between the two complete thoughts; others have only a comma.

Correct each run-on by using (1) a period and capital letter, (2) a comma and a joining word, or (3) a semicolon. Do not use the same method of correction for every sentence.

_____ 1. The supermarket needs to hire more cashiers customers must stand in long checkout lines just to buy a few groceries.

_____ 2. The news reporter said the snowstorm would dump a foot of snow on our city, but all we saw were a few flurries.

_____ 3. Metal detectors are being installed in many high schools this will prevent students from bringing weapons to school.

_____ 4. Critics said the new movie was horrible the large crowd in the theater seemed to disagree.

_____ 5. Dust and cat fur covered the floor of the old attic it was an allergy sufferer's nightmare.

_____ 6. Kendra looked everywhere for her car keys they turned out to be in her pocket.

_____ 7. Honeybees can communicate to each other by "dancing" their movements tell other bees where to find nectar-filled flowers.

_____ 8. The volcano destroyed the surrounding forest thousands of old trees were snapped like dry twigs.

_____ 9. Ken's new dog has a bad habit it likes to eat leather shoes.

_____ 10. Leeches are unpleasant wormlike creatures that drink blood they can also help doctors treat severe injuries.

NAME: _____

DATE: _____

MASTERY TEST 5 | Run-Ons

In the space provided, write *R-O* beside run-on sentences. Write *C* beside the one sentence that is punctuated correctly. Some of the run-ons have no punctuation between the two complete thoughts; others have only a comma.

Correct each run-on by using (1) a period and a capital letter, (2) a comma and a joining word, or (3) a semicolon. Do not use the same method of correction for every sentence.

_____ 1. The cable company increased rates twice this year customers have threatened to cancel their service.

_____ 2. Bill wanted to arrive for the interview early he missed his bus.

_____ 3. The salesperson said the used car was in perfect shape the engine was dotted with rust.

_____ 4. Wind howled through the trees rain pelted loudly against the windows of our house.

_____ 5. A pen exploded in the washing machine all Sara's clothes were stained in blue ink.

_____ 6. In the 1300s, one-third of Europe's population was killed by the bubonic plague this highly contagious disease was spread by fleas.

_____ 7. Kathy spilled soda on her expensive new cell phone, and then it stopped working.

_____ 8. Angry basketball fans yelled at the referee his mistakes cost the team at least six points.

_____ 9. Security cameras filmed the jewelry store robbery police have not been able to catch the thieves.

_____ 10. Today, the average American woman can expect to live seventy-nine years the lifespan of the average man is just seventy-five.

Sentence Variety I

This chapter will show you how to write effective and varied sentences. You'll learn more about two techniques—subordination and coordination—you can use to expand simple sentences, making them more interesting and expressive. You'll also reinforce what you have learned in Chapters 5 and 6 about how subordination and coordination can help you correct fragments and run-ons in your writing.

Four Traditional Sentence Patterns

Sentences in English are traditionally described as *simple, compound, complex,* or *compound-complex.* Each is explained below.

The Simple Sentence

A simple sentence has a single subject-verb combination.

> Children play.
>
> The game ended early.
>
> My car stalled three times last week.
>
> The lake has been polluted by several neighboring streams.

A simple sentence may have more than one subject:

> Lola and Tony drove home.
>
> The wind and water dried my hair.

or more than one verb:

> The children smiled and waved at us.
>
> The lawn mower smoked and sputtered.

or several subjects and verbs:

> Manny, Moe, and Jack lubricated my car, replaced the oil filter, and cleaned
> the spark plugs.

Practice

1

On separate paper, write:

> Three sentences, each with a single subject and verb
>
> Three sentences, each with a single subject and a double verb
>
> Three sentences, each with a double subject and a single verb

In each case, underline the subject once and the verb twice. (See pages 67–68 if necessary for more information on subjects and verbs.)

The Compound Sentence

A compound, or "double," sentence is made up of two (or more) simple sentences. The two complete statements in a compound sentence are usually connected by a comma plus a joining word (*and, but, for, or, nor, so, yet*).

A compound sentence is used when you want to give equal weight to two closely related ideas. The technique of showing that ideas have equal importance is called *coordination*.

Following are some compound sentences. Each sentence contains two ideas that the writer considers equal in importance.

> The rain increased, so the officials canceled the game.
>
> Martha wanted to go shopping, but Fred refused to drive her.
>
> Hollis was watching television in the family room, and April was upstairs on the phone.
>
> I had to give up woodcarving, for my arthritis had become very painful.

Combine the following pairs of simple sentences into compound sentences. Use a comma and a logical joining word (*and, but, for, so*) to connect each pair.

HINT If you are not sure what *and, but, for,* and *so* mean, review pages 108–109.

Practice

2

EXAMPLE

- We hung up the print.
- The wall still looked bare.

  We hung up the print, but the wall still looked bare.

1. • My cold grew worse.
   • I decided to see a doctor.

   _____
   _____

2. • My uncle always ignores me.
   • My aunt gives me kisses and presents.

   _____
   _____

3. • We played softball in the afternoon.
   • We went to a movie in the evening.

   _____
   _____

4. • I invited Rico to sleep overnight.
   • He wanted to go home.

   _____
   _____

5. • Police raided the club.
   • They had gotten a tip about illegal drugs for sale.

   _____
   _____

On separate paper, write five compound sentences of your own about the photo below. Use a different joining word (*and, but, for, or, nor, so, yet*) to connect the two complete ideas in each sentence.

The Complex Sentence

A complex sentence consists of a simple sentence (a complete statement) and a statement that begins with a dependent word.* Here is a list of common dependent words:

Dependent Words		
after	if, even if	when, whenever
although, though	in order that	where, wherever
as	since	whether
because	that, so that	which, whichever
before	unless	while
even though	until	who
how	what, whatever	whose

A complex sentence is used when you want to emphasize one idea over another in a sentence. Look at the following complex sentence:

Because I forgot the time, I missed the final exam.

---

*The two parts of a complex sentence are sometimes called an independent clause and a dependent clause. A *clause* is simply a word group that contains a subject and a verb. An *independent clause* expresses a complete thought and can stand alone. A *dependent clause* does not express a complete thought in itself and "depends on" the independent clause to complete its meaning. Dependent clauses always begin with a dependent or subordinating word.

The idea that the writer wants to emphasize here—*I missed the final exam*—is expressed as a complete thought. The less important idea—*Because I forgot the time*—is subordinated to the complete thought. The technique of giving one idea less emphasis than another is called *subordination.*

Following are other examples of complex sentences. In each case, the part starting with the dependent word is the less emphasized part of the sentence.

While Aisha was eating breakfast, she began to feel sick.

I checked my money *before* I invited Pedro for lunch.

When Jerry lost his temper, he also lost his job.

Although I practiced for three months, I failed my driving test.

Use logical dependent words to combine the following pairs of simple sentences into complex sentences. Place a comma after a dependent statement when it starts the sentence.

EXAMPLES

- I obtained a credit card.
- I began spending money recklessly.
  When I obtained a credit card, I began spending money recklessly.

- Alan dressed the turkey.
- His brother greased the roasting pan.
  Alan dressed the turkey while his brother greased the roasting pan.

1. • The instructor announced the quiz.
   • The class groaned.

   _____

   _____

2. • Gene could not fit any more groceries into his cart.
   • He decided to go to the checkout counter.

   _____

   _____

3. • Your car is out of commission.
   • You should take it to Otto's Transmission.

   _____

   _____

4. • I received a raise at work.
    • I called my boss to say thank you.

    _____

5. • We owned four cats and a dog.
    • No one would rent us an apartment.

    _____

    _____

Practice

5

Rewrite the following sentences, using subordination rather than coordination. Include a comma when a dependent statement starts a sentence.

EXAMPLE

The hair dryer was not working right, so I returned it to the store.

Because the hair dryer was not working right, I returned it

to the store.

1. Ruth turned on the large window fan, but the room remained hot.

    _____

    _____

2. The plumber repaired the water heater, so we can take showers again.

    _____

    _____

3. I washed the sheets and towels, and I scrubbed the bathroom floor.

    _____

    _____

4. You should go to a doctor, for your chest cold may get worse.

    _____

    _____

5. The fish tank broke, and guppies were flopping all over the carpet.

    _____

    _____

Combine the following simple sentences into complex sentences. Omit repeated words. Use the dependent words *who, which,* or *that.*

HINTS

a. The word *who* refers to persons.
b. The word *which* refers to things.
c. The word *that* refers to persons or things.

Use commas around the dependent statement only if it seems to interrupt the flow of thought in the sentence. (See pages 358–359.)

EXAMPLES

- Clyde picked up a hitchhiker.
- The hitchhiker was traveling around the world.

  Clyde picked up a hitchhiker who was traveling around the world.

- Larry is a sleepwalker.
- Larry is my brother.

  Larry, who is my brother, is a sleepwalker.

1. • The magazine article was about abortion.
   • The article made me very angry.

   _____

   _____

2. • The woodshed has collapsed.
   • I built the woodshed myself.

   _____

   _____

3. • The power drill is missing.
   • I bought the power drill at half price.

   _____

   _____

4. • Rita Haber was indicted for bribery.
   • Rita Haber is our mayor.

   _____

5. • The chicken pies contained dangerous preservatives.
   • We ate the chicken pies.

   _____

   _____

Practice

7

On separate paper, write eight complex sentences, using, in turn, the dependent words *unless, if, after, because, when, who, which,* and *that.*

The Compound-Complex Sentence

A compound-complex sentence is made up of two (or more) simple sentences and one (or more) dependent statements. In the following examples, a solid line is under the simple sentences and a dotted line is under the dependent statements.

When the power line snapped, Jack was listening to the stereo, and Linda was reading in bed.

After I returned to school following a long illness, the math teacher gave me makeup work, but the history instructor made me drop her course.

Practice

8

Read through each sentence to get a sense of its overall meaning. Then insert a logical joining word (*and, or, but, for,* or *so*) and a logical dependent word (*because, since, when,* or *although*).

1. _____ he suffered so much during hay fever season, Pete bought

   an air conditioner, _____ he swallowed allergy pills regularly.

2. _____ I put on my new flannel shirt, I discovered that a button

   was missing, _____ I angrily went looking for a replacement

   button in the sewing basket.

3. _____ the computer was just repaired, the screen keeps freezing,

   _____ I have to restart the program.

4. _____ I have lived all my life on the East Coast, I felt uncomfortable during a West Coast vacation, _____ I kept thinking that the ocean was on the wrong side.

5. _____ water condensation continues in your basement, either you should buy a dehumidifier _____ you should cover the masonry walls with waterproof paint.

On separate paper, write five compound-complex sentences.

Review of Subordination and Coordination

Subordination and coordination are ways of showing the exact relationship of ideas within a sentence. Through **subordination** we show that one idea is less important than another. When we subordinate, we use dependent words like *when, although, while, because,* and *after.* (A list of common dependent words has been given on page 128.) Through **coordination** we show that ideas are of equal importance. When we coordinate, we use the words *and, but, for, or, nor, so, yet.*

www.mhhe.com/langan

Use subordination or coordination to combine the following groups of simple sentences into one or more longer sentences. Be sure to omit repeated words. Since various combinations are possible, you might want to jot down several combinations on separate paper. Then read them aloud to find the combination that sounds best.

Keep in mind that, very often, the relationship among ideas in a sentence will be clearer when subordination rather than coordination is used.

EXAMPLE

- My car does not start on cold mornings.
- I think the battery needs to be replaced.
- I already had it recharged once.
- I don't think charging it again would help.

Because my car does not start on cold mornings, I think the battery
needs to be replaced. I already had it recharged once, so I don't think
charging it again would help.

> **COMMA HINTS**
>
> a. Use a comma at the end of a word group that starts with a dependent word (as in "Because my car does not start on cold mornings, . . .").
>
> b. Use a comma between independent word groups connected by *and, but, for, or, nor, so, yet* (as in "I already had it recharged once, so . . .").

1. • Louise used a dandruff shampoo.
   • She still had dandruff.
   • She decided to see a dermatologist.

   _____

   _____

   _____

2. • Omar's parents want him to be a doctor.
   • Omar wants to be a salesman.
   • He impresses people with his charm.

   _____

   _____

   _____

3. • The instructor conducted a discussion period.
   • Jack sat at his desk with his head down.
   • He did not want the instructor to call on him.
   • He had not read the assignment.

   _____

   _____

   _____

   _____

- At the end of the day, the store has made money.
- At the end of the day, the manager is happy.
- At the end of the day, the salespeople feel like quitting.

Review Test 2

Combine each group of short sentences into one sentence. Various combinations are possible. Choose the combination that reads most smoothly and clearly and that sounds most appropriate in the context of surrounding sentences. In combining short sentences into one sentence, omit repeated words where necessary. Use separate paper.

Life in Winter

- Many people think winter is a dead season.
- It is actually full of hidden life.

- For instance, many insects die in autumn.
- They leave life behind in the form of eggs.

- The eggs hatch the next spring.
- Millions of young insects will emerge.
- They will continue the life cycle.

- Other animals bury themselves alive.
- They can escape winter's cold.

- Frogs and turtles dig into the mud.
- They enter a state of hibernation.

- The pond freezes.
- The frogs and turtles remain alive.

- Woodchucks also go into a deep, months-long sleep.
- Winter is on its way.

- The woodchuck enters its den.
- This happens when it is ready to hibernate.
- It rolls into a tight ball.

- The woodchuck's heart slows to five beats a minute.
- It normally beats eighty times a minute.
- This happens until spring returns.

- The winter may be long and bitter.
- Life goes on.

DATE: _____

Sentence Variety I

Combine each group of short sentences into one sentence. Various combinations are possible. Choose the combination that reads most smoothly and clearly and that sounds most appropriate in the context of surrounding sentences. Use separate paper.

> HINT In combining short sentences into one sentence, omit repeated words where necessary.

Cocoa and Donut

- The little boy sat in a high chair.
- He watched his father dunk a white sugar donut into a cup of coffee.
- He watched his father take a bite of the wet donut.

- The boy then picked up a piece of white sugar donut.
- The piece of donut was on his high-chair tray.
- He did not put the donut into his mouth.

- The boy pushed the donut into the cup of cocoa on the tray.
- He did this after he made sure his father wasn't watching.
- He watched it sink.

- Then he pushed on the donut.
- He did so until cocoa flowed over the top of the cup.
- It ran onto the tray.
- It dripped onto a white linen tablecloth.

- Then the boy pulled out the soggy piece of donut from the cup.
- He jammed it into his mouth.

NAME: _____

DATE: _____

MASTERY TEST 2 | # Sentence Variety I

Combine each group of short sentences into one sentence. Various combinations are possible. Choose the combination that reads most smoothly and clearly and that sounds most appropriate in the context of surrounding sentences. Use separate paper.

> **HINT** In combining short sentences into one sentence, omit repeated words where necessary.

Jack Alone

- Jack worked a long day.
- The work was as a delivery man for United Parcel.
- He entered his apartment, hoping to relax.

- He ate his takeout pizza.
- He took off his heavy brown uniform.
- He put on his comfortable flannel pajamas.

- Jack then shuffled back to the kitchen.
- He boiled water.
- He made a large cup of tea.

- Jack added a tablespoon of honey to the tea.
- He also got a few cookies.

- Jack might feel lonely later.
- He was relaxed and comfortable now.
- He was happy to be by himself.

Standard English Verbs

8

Introductory Activity

Underline what you think is the correct form of the verb in each pair of
sentences below.

That radio station once (play, played) top-forty hits.

It now (play, plays) classical music.

When Jean was a little girl, she (hope, hoped) to become a movie star.

Now she (hope, hopes) to be accepted at law school.

At first, my father (juggle, juggled) with balls of yarn.

Now that he is an expert, he (juggle, juggles) raw eggs.

On the basis of the examples above, see if you can complete the following
statements.

1. The first sentence in each pair refers to an action in (past time, the
   present time), and the regular verb has an _____ ending.

2. The second sentence in each pair refers to an action in (past time, the
   present time), and the regular verb has an _____ ending.

Answers are on page 562.

Many people have grown up in communities where nonstandard verb forms are used in everyday life. Such nonstandard forms include *they be, it done, we has, you was, she don't,* and *it ain't.* Community dialects have richness and power but are a drawback in college and the world at large, where standard English verb forms must be used. Standard English helps ensure clear communication among English-speaking people everywhere, and it is especially important in the world of work.

This chapter compares the community dialect and the standard English forms of a regular verb and three common irregular verbs.

Regular Verbs: Dialect and Standard Forms

The chart below compares community dialect (nonstandard) and standard English forms of the regular verb *talk.*

Talk			
Community Dialect **(Do not use in your writing)**		*Standard English* **(Use for clear communication)**	
Present Tense			
I talks	we talks	I talk	we talk
you talks	you talks	you talk	you talk
he, she, it talk	they talk	he, she, it talks	they talk
Past Tense			
I talk	we talk	I talked	we talked
you talk	you talk	you talked	you talked
he, she, it talk	they talk	he, she, it talked	they talked

One of the most common nonstandard forms results from dropping the endings of regular verbs. For example, people might say "Rose work until ten o'clock tonight" instead of "Rose work*s* until ten o'clock tonight." Or they'll say "I work overtime yesterday" instead of "I work*ed* overtime yesterday." To avoid such nonstandard usage, memorize the forms shown above for the regular verb *talk.* Then do the activities that follow. These activities will help you make it a habit to include verb endings in your writing.

Present Tense Endings

The verb ending *-s* or *-es* is needed with a regular verb in the present tense when the subject is *he, she, it,* or any one person or thing.

He	He lifts weights.
She	She runs.
It	It amazes me.
One person	Their son Ted swims.
One person	Their daughter Terry dances.
One thing	Their house jumps at night with all the exercise.

All but one of the ten sentences that follow need *-s* or *-es* endings. Cross out the nonstandard verb forms and write the standard forms in the spaces provided. Mark the one sentence that needs no change with a *C*.

Practice

1

www.mhhe.com/langan

EXAMPLE

_____*ends*_____   The sale ~~end~~ tomorrow.

_____   1. Renée hate it when I criticize her singing.

_____   2. Whenever my sister tries to tell a joke, she always mess it up.

_____   3. Ice cream feel good going down a sore throat.

_____   4. Frank cover his ears every time his baby sister cries.

_____   5. "Dinner sure smell good," said Fran as she walked into the kitchen.

_____   6. My brother wants to be an astronaut so he can see stars.

_____   7. The picture on our television set blur whenever there is a storm.

_____   8. My mother think women should get equal pay for equal work.

_____   9. Sometimes Alonso pretend that he is living in a penthouse.

_____   10. It seem as if we are working more and more but getting paid less and less.

Practice

2

Rewrite the short selection below, adding present tense -*s* verb endings wherever needed.

Charlotte behave rudely when she speak on her cell phone. First of all, she answer the phone anytime it ring, even at a restaurant or the movies. Then she raise her voice and act as if the caller is sitting right next to her. Sometimes she wave her hands or laugh loudly. She never notice how people roll their eyes at her. She even ask others near her to be quiet while she talk. If she keep this up, no one will go anywhere with her—unless she leave the phone at home.

_____

_____

_____

_____

_____

_____

_____

_____

_____

_____

_____

_____

_____

_____

_____

_____

Past Tense Endings

The verb ending -*d* or -*ed* is needed with a regular verb in the past tense.

Yesterday we finished painting the house.

I completed the paper an hour before class.

Fred's car stalled on his way to work this morning.

www.mhhe.com/langan

All but one of the ten sentences that follow need -*d* or -*ed* endings. Cross out the nonstandard verb forms and write the standard forms in the spaces provided. Mark the one sentence that needs no change with a *C*.

EXAMPLE

jumped   The cat ~~jump~~ on my lap when I sat down.

_____   1. As the burglar alarm went off, three men race out the door.

_____   2. Jenna's new lipstick was so red that it glow in the dark.

_____   3. Stan smelled gas when he walk into the apartment.

_____   4. As soon as the pilot sight the runway, he turned on his landing lights.

_____   5. While the bear stare hungrily at him, the tourist reached for his camera.

_____   6. Aliya studied for three hours and then decide to get some sleep.

_____   7. Just as Miss Muffet seated herself, a large spider joined her.

_____   8. José hurried to cash his paycheck because he need money for the weekend.

_____   9. The waiter dropped the tray with a loud crash; bits of broken glass scatter all over the floor.

_____   10. A customer who twisted his ankle in the diner's parking lot decide to sue.

Rewrite this selection, adding past tense -*d* or -*ed* verb endings where needed.

Bill's boss shout at Bill. Feeling bad, Bill went home and curse his wife. Then his wife scream at their son. Angry himself, the son went out and cruelly tease a little girl who live next door until she wail. Bad feelings were pass on as one person wound the next with ugly words. No one manage to break the vicious circle.

_____

_____

_____

_____

_____

_____

Three Common Irregular Verbs: Dialect and Standard Forms

The following charts compare the nonstandard and standard dialects of the common irregular verbs *be, have,* and *do.* (For more on irregular verbs, see the next chapter, beginning on page 157.)

Be

Community Dialect **(Do not use in your writing)**		*Standard English* **(Use for clear communication)**	
Present Tense			
I be (*or* is)	we be	I am	we are
you be	you be	you are	you are
he, she, it be	they be	he, she, it is	they are
Past Tense			
I were	we was	I was	we were
you was	you was	you were	you were
he, she, it were	they was	he, she, it was	they were

Have

Community Dialect **(Do not use in your writing)**		*Standard English* **(Use for clear communication)**	
Present Tense			
I has	we has	I have	we have
you has	you has	you have	you have
he, she, it have	they has	he, she, it has	they have
Past Tense			
I has	we has	I had	we had
you has	you has	you had	you had
he, she, it have	they has	he, she, it had	they had

Do

Community Dialect
(Do not use in your writing)

Standard English
(Use for clear communication)

Present Tense

I does	we does	I do	we do
you does	you does	you do	you do
he, she, it do	they does	he, she, it does	they do

Past Tense

I done	we done	I did	we did
you done	you done	you did	you did
he, she, it done	they done	he, she, it did	they did

TIP   Many people have trouble with one negative form of *do*. They will say, for example, "She don't listen" instead of "She doesn't listen," or they will say "This pen don't work" instead of "This pen doesn't work." Be careful to avoid the common mistake of using *don't* instead of *doesn't*.

Underline the standard form of the irregular verb *be, have,* or *do*.

Practice

5

1. This week, my Aunt Charlotte (have, has) a dentist's appointment.

2. She (does, do) not enjoy going to the dentist.

3. She (is, are) always frightened by the shiny instruments.

4. The drills (is, are) the worst thing in the office.

5. When Aunt Charlotte (was, were) a little girl, she (have, had) a bad experience at the dentist's.

6. The dentist told her he (was, were) going to pull out all her teeth.

7. Aunt Charlotte (do, did) not realize that he (was, were) only joking.

8. Her parents (was, were) unprepared for her screams of terror.

9. Now, she (has, had) a bad attitude toward dentists.

10. She refuses to keep an appointment unless I (am, are) with her in the waiting room.

Cross out the nonstandard verb form in each sentence. Then write the standard form of *be, have,* or *do* in the space provided.

_____ 1. If it be not raining tomorrow, we're going camping.

_____ 2. You is invited to join us.

_____ 3. You has to bring your own sleeping bag and flashlight.

_____ 4. It don't hurt to bring a raincoat also, in case of a sudden shower.

_____ 5. The stars is beautiful on a warm summer night.

_____ 6. Last year we have a great time on a family camping trip.

_____ 7. We done all the cooking ourselves.

_____ 8. The food tasted good even though it have some dead leaves in it.

_____ 9. Then we discovered that we has no insect repellent.

_____ 10. When we got home, we was covered with mosquito bites.

Fill in each blank with the standard form of *be, have,* or *do.*

My mother sings alto in our church choir. She _____ to go to choir practice every Friday night and _____ expected to know all the music. If she _____ not know her part, the other choir members _____ things like glare at her and _____ likely to make nasty comments, she says. Last weekend, my mother _____ houseguests and _____ not have time to learn all the notes. The music _____ very difficult, and she thought the other people _____ going to make fun of her. But they _____ very understanding when she told them that she _____ laryngitis and couldn't make a sound.

Review Test 1

Underline the standard verb form.

1. Paul (pound, pounded) the mashed potatoes until they turned into glue.

2. The velvety banana (rest, rests) on the shiny counter.

3. My neighbor's daughter (have, has) a brand-new Toyota.

4. It (is, be) fire-engine red with black leather upholstery.

5. The tree in the backyard (have, had) to be cut down.

6. When Rashid (talk, talks) about his ex-wife, his eyes grow hard and cold.

7. Every time my heart (skip, skips) a beat, I worry about my health.

8. My friend Pat (do, does) everything at the last minute.

9. The pattern on the wallpaper (look, looks) like fuzzy brown spiders marching in rows.

10. My hands (tremble, trembled) when I gave my speech in front of the class.

Review Test 2

Cross out the nonstandard verb forms in the sentences that follow. Then write the standard English verb forms in the space above, as shown.

EXAMPLE
watches   _play_
She ~~watch~~ closely while the children ~~plays~~ in the water.

1. The stores was all closed by the time the movie were over.

2. If you does your assignment on time, that instructor are going to like you.

3. The boxer pull his punches; the fight were fixed.

4. The tires is whitewalls; they be very good-looking.

5. He typically start to write a research paper the night before it be due.

6. It don't matter to him whether he have to stay up all night.

7. Jeannette anchor the relay team, since she be the fastest runner.

8. I done Bill a favor that I hope he don't forget.

9. Last year I save all my money and buy a Macintosh computer.

10. I add the figures again and again, but I still weren't able to understand the bank statement.

NAME: _____

DATE: _____

MASTERY TEST 1 | Standard English Verbs

Underline the correct words in the parentheses.

1. The radio announcer said that traffic (is, are) tied up for six miles because of an accident that just (happen, happened) on the expressway.

2. My new pen (scratch, scratches) when I write with it; it (make, makes) little cuts in the paper.

3. Before I (mail, mailed) the letter, the postal rate went up, so I (need, needed) an extra stamp.

4. Rodrigo (have, has) a new tuxedo that (make, makes) him look just like a movie star.

5. They (do, does) not plan to give a New Year's Eve party this year, for they (have, has) painful memories of last year's.

6. Tim (is, be) terrific at home repairs; for example, he (fix, fixes) broken appliances just like a professional.

7. Just as Stanley (walk, walked) around the corner, he saw someone trying to steal his bicycle, so he (yell, yelled) for the police.

8. Little Danny (pile, piled) the blocks into a tower, but it (collapse, collapsed) with a loud crash, scattering all over the floor.

9. We (suspect, suspected) from the start that it (was, were) the neighbor's boy who took our lawn furniture.

10. My two sisters (was, were) thrilled when I (turn, turned) up with three tickets to the rock concert.

Standard English Verbs MASTERY TEST 2

Cross out the nonstandard verb form and write the correct form in the space provided.

EXAMPLE

_____seems_____   The job offer seem too good to be true.

_____   1. When I was learning how to drive, I strip the gears on my father's car.

_____   2. My parents is going to throw me a big party when I graduate.

_____   3. Rhonda prefer watching YouTube to watching television.

_____   4. Vince do well on every exam he takes.

_____   5. Lucille change into comfortable clothes right after she gets home from a day of work.

_____   6. I remember how my mittens used to steam when I place them on the living room radiator.

_____   7. It was so cold that my breath turn into sharp white puffs of smoke when I exhaled.

_____   8. When Ida have her work breaks during the day, she often reads a magazine.

_____   9. Tea contain so much caffeine that it stimulates some people more than coffee.

_____   10. When I were little, my father would punish me just for expressing my opinion.

NAME: _____

DATE: _____

MASTERY TEST 3 Standard English Verbs

PART 1

Fill in each blank with the appropriate standard verb form of *be, have,* or *do* in present or past tense.

People _____ really funny at amusement parks. They _____ to prove that
           1   2
they _____ absolutely fearless, so they _____ crazy things such as stand up
       3   4
while the roller coaster _____ on its way downhill at ninety miles per hour. A
                                 5
normally careful driver _____ accidents on purpose; he _____ this to see how
                          6   7
many cars he can hit in the Demolition Derby. I wonder if our parents _____
                                                            8
equally crazy things when they _____ kids and needed to prove to the world that
                                      9
they _____ courage.
       10

PART 2

Fill in each blank with the appropriate form of the regular verb shown in parentheses. Use present or past tense as needed.

When Joanne (*rush*) _____, she often gets into trouble. Last Monday, while
                                  11
in a hurry to catch her train, she (*park*) _____ her car too close to a shiny green
                                      12
Camaro that was in the next space on the lot. When she (*arrive*) _____ at the sta-
                                              13
tion in the afternoon and (*open*) _____ her car door, Joanne (*realize*) _____ she
                               14   15
could not back out of the parking space without hitting the other car. In addition,
its driver was waiting impatiently and (*scowl*) _____ as she (*watch*) _____
                                               16   17
Joanne struggling with the wheel. Joanne finally got out of the space, but she
(*scrape*) _____ a two-inch strip off the Camaro's fender. The angry driver of
                18
the other car (*calm*) _____ down only when Joanne (*agree*) _____ to pay.
                          19   20

NAME: _____

DATE: _____

Standard English Verbs MASTERY TEST 4

PART 1

Fill in each blank with the appropriate standard verb form of *be, have,* or *do* in the present or past tense.

My cousin Rita _____ determined to lose ten pounds, so she _____ put
        1   2
herself on a rigid diet that _____ not allow her to eat anything she enjoys. Last
                              3
weekend while the family _____ at Aunt Agatha's house for dinner, all Rita
                          4
_____ to eat _____ a can of Diet Delight peaches. We _____ convinced that
  5   6   7
Rita meant business when she joined an exercise club whose members _____ to
                                                                      8
work out on enormous machines and _____ fifty sit-ups just to get started. If Rita
                                    9
succeeds, we _____ going to be proud.
            10

PART 2

Fill in each blank with the appropriate form of the regular verb shown in parentheses. Use present or past tense as needed.

Have you ever (*notice*) _____ what (*happen*) _____ at a children's
                          11   12
playground? Very often one child (*struggle*) _____ with another to be first
                                              13
on the sliding board, while a third child (*compete*) _____ with a fourth for the
                                                      14
sandbox. Meanwhile, each parent (*wait*) _____ patiently on a nearby park bench
                                        15
and (*ignore*) _____ his or her offspring. Just yesterday, I saw a young father
              16
whose daughter had (*drag*) _____ him to the playground. He (*stare*) _____
                            17   18
at his watch while she (*scream*) _____ happily from the top of the jungle gym.
                                 19
He must have been counting the minutes until they (*return*) _____ home.
                                                             20

155

Irregular Verbs

Introductory Activity

You may already have a sense of which common English verbs are regular and which are not. To test yourself, fill in the past tense and past participle of the verbs below. Five are regular verbs and so take *-d* or *-ed* in the past tense and past participle. For these verbs, write *R* under *Verb Type* and then write their past tense and past participle verb forms. Five are irregular verbs and will probably not sound right when you try to add *-d* or *-ed*. For these verbs, write *I* under *Verb Type*. Also, see if you can write in their irregular verb forms.

Present	Verb Type	Past	Past Participle
fall	*I*	*fell*	*fallen*
1. scream			
2. write			
3. steal			
4. ask			
5. kiss			
6. choose			
7. ride			
8. chew			
9. think			
10. dance			

Answers are on page 562.

A Brief Review of Regular Verbs

Every verb has four principal parts: present, past, past participle, and present participle. These parts can be used to build all the verb tenses (the times shown by a verb).

Most verbs in English are regular. The past and past participle of a regular verb are formed by adding *-d* or *-ed* to the present. The *past participle* is the form of the verb used with the helping verbs *have, has,* or *had* (or some form of *be* with passive verbs, which are explained on pages 196–197). The *present participle* is formed by adding *-ing* to the present. Here are the principal forms of some regular verbs:

Present	Past	Past Participle	Present Participle
laugh	laughed	laughed	laughing
ask	asked	asked	asking
touch	touched	touched	touching
decide	decided	decided	deciding
explode	exploded	exploded	exploding

List of Irregular Verbs

Irregular verbs have irregular forms in the past tense and past participle. For example, the past tense of the irregular verb *grow* is *grew;* the past participle is *grown.*

Almost everyone has some degree of trouble with irregular verbs. When you are unsure about the form of a verb, you can check the following list of irregular verbs. (The present participle is not shown on this list, because it is formed simply by adding *-ing* to the base form of the verb.) Or you can check a dictionary, which gives the principal parts of irregular verbs.

Present	Past	Past Participle
arise	arose	arisen
awake	awoke *or* awaked	awoke *or* awaked
be (am, are, is)	was (were)	been
become	became	become
begin	began	begun
bend	bent	bent
bite	bit	bitten
blow	blew	blown

Present	Past	Past Participle
break	broke	broken
bring	brought	brought
build	built	built
burst	burst	burst
buy	bought	bought
catch	caught	caught
choose	chose	chosen
come	came	come
cost	cost	cost
cut	cut	cut
do (does)	did	done
draw	drew	drawn
drink	drank	drunk
drive	drove	driven
eat	ate	eaten
fall	fell	fallen
feed	fed	fed
feel	felt	felt
fight	fought	fought
find	found	found
fly	flew	flown
freeze	froze	frozen
get	got	got *or* gotten
give	gave	given
go (goes)	went	gone
grow	grew	grown
have (has)	had	had
hear	heard	heard
hide	hid	hidden
hold	held	held
hurt	hurt	hurt
keep	kept	kept
know	knew	known
lay	laid	laid
lead	led	led

Present	Past	Past Participle
leave	left	left
lend	lent	lent
let	let	let
lie	lay	lain
light	lit	lit
lose	lost	lost
make	made	made
meet	met	met
pay	paid	paid
ride	rode	ridden
ring	rang	rung
rise	rose	risen
run	ran	run
say	said	said
see	saw	seen
sell	sold	sold
send	sent	sent
shake	shook	shaken
shrink	shrank *or* shrunk	shrunk *or* shrunken
shut	shut	shut
sing	sang	sung
sit	sat	sat
sleep	slept	slept
speak	spoke	spoken
spend	spent	spent
stand	stood	stood
steal	stole	stolen
stick	stuck	stuck
sting	stung	stung
swear	swore	sworn
swim	swam	swum
take	took	taken
teach	taught	taught
tear	tore	torn
tell	told	told

Present	Past	Past Participle
think	thought	thought
wake	woke *or* waked	woken *or* waked
wear	wore	worn
win	won	won
write	wrote	written

Practice

1

Cross out the incorrect verb form in the following sentences. Then write the correct form of the verb in the space provided.

EXAMPLE

began   When the mud slide started, the whole neighborhood ~~begun~~ going downhill.

_____ 1. The winner of the reality show has ate three bowls of juicy worms.

_____ 2. The mechanic done an expensive valve job on my engine without getting my permission.

_____ 3. Sheri has wore that ring since the day Clyde bought it for her.

_____ 4. She has wrote a paper that will make you roar with laughter.

_____ 5. The gas station attendant gived him the wrong change.

_____ 6. My sister be at school when a stranger came asking for her at our home.

_____ 7. The basketball team has broke the school record for most losses in a year.

_____ 8. Because I had lended him the money, I had a natural concern about what he did with it.

_____ 9. I seen that stray dog nosing around the yard yesterday.

_____ 10. I knowed her face from somewhere, but I couldn't remember just where.

Practice

2

For each of the italicized verbs in the following sentences, fill in the three missing forms in the order shown in the box:

> a. Present tense, which takes an -s ending when the subject is *he, she, it,* or any *one person or thing* (see page 145)
> b. Past tense
> c. Past participle—the form that goes with the helping verb *have, has,* or *had*

EXAMPLE

My little nephew loves to *break* things. Every Christmas he (a) *breaks* his new toys the minute they're unwrapped. Last year he (b) *broke* five toys in seven minutes and then went on to smash his family's new china platter. His mother says he won't be happy until he has (c) *broken* their hearts.

1. Mary Beth wears contact lenses in order to *see* well. In fact, she (a) _____ so poorly without the lenses that the world is a multicolored blur. Once, when she lost one lens, she thought she (b) _____ a frog in the sink. She had really (c) _____ a lump of green soap.

2. When I was younger, I used to hate it when my gym class had to *choose* sides for a baseball game. Each captain, of course, (a) _____ the better players first. Since I was nearsighted and couldn't see a fly ball until it fell on my head, I would often have to wait half the period until one or the other captain (b) _____ me. If I had had my way, I would have (c) _____ to play chess.

3. My father loves to *take* pictures. Whenever we go on vacation, he (a) _____ at least ten rolls of film along. Last year, he (b) _____ more than two hundred pictures of the same mountain scenery. Only after he had (c) _____ his last shot were we allowed to climb the mountain.

4. Instructors must love to *speak* to their classes. My English instructor (a) _____ so much that he has to get a drink of water midway through his lecture. Last Wednesday, he (b) _____ for the entire class period. I guess he never heard that old expression "Speak only when you're (c) _____ to."

5. Our next-door neighbor's pet poodle loves to *swim*. When there is no lake or pond handy, she (a) _____ in the family bathtub. Two summers ago, Fifi (b) _____ across the river in which the family was fishing. She won't be satisfied until she has (c) _____ the English Channel.

6. Convertibles are not practical, but they are fun to *drive*. My cousin has a sky-blue Chevrolet convertible which she (a) _____ to work. One day she (b) _____ with the top down and then forgot to put it back up again. That night it rained, and the seat was so wet the next day that she has (c) _____ with the top up ever since.

7. Annabelle loves buying new things to *wear*. She (a) _____ a different outfit every day of the year. Last year, she never (b) _____ the same clothing twice. She often complains that she gets tired of her clothes long before they're (c) _____ out.

8. My eight-year-old nephew likes to *blow* up balloons. Every year he (a) _____ up several dozen for his parents' New Year's Eve party. Last year, he (b) _____ up fifty balloons, including one in the shape of an American flag. When he tiptoed downstairs at midnight, he was thrilled to see all the guests saluting the balloon he had (c) _____ up.

9. Every year, I can't wait for summer vacation to *begin*. As soon as it (a) _____, I can get to work on all the things around the house that I had to ignore during school. This past May, the minute my exams were over, I (b) _____ cleaning out the garage, painting the windowsills, and building a bookcase. I must have (c) _____ half a dozen projects. Unfortunately, it's now Labor Day, and I haven't finished any of them.

10. We always have trouble getting our younger son, Teddy, to stop watching television and *go* to sleep. He never (a) _____ to his room until 10 or 11 P.M. In the past, when he finally (b) _____ upstairs, we did not check on him, since there was no TV set in his room. The night we finally did decide to look in on Teddy, we found him reading *TV Guide* with a flashlight under the covers and told him things had (c) _____ too far.

Troublesome Irregular Verbs

Three common irregular verbs that often give people trouble are *be, have,* and *do.* See pages 148–149 for a discussion of these verbs. Three sets of other irregular verbs that can lead to difficulties are *lie-lay, sit-set,* and *rise-raise.*

Irregular Verbs MASTERY TEST 1

Underline the correct word in the parentheses.

1. Juan had (wrote, written) me five times before the letters stopped.

2. Did you see the damage that maniac (did, done) to the laundromat?

3. The fever made me hallucinate, and I (saw, seen) monkeys at the foot of my bed.

4. After dicing the vegetables, Sarah (freezed, froze) them.

5. I (drank, drunk) at least six cups of coffee while working on the paper.

6. That last commercial (came, come) close to making me scream.

7. The foreman asked why I had (went, gone) home early from work the day before.

8. I should have (wore, worn) heavier clothes to the picnic.

9. If I hadn't (threw, thrown) away the receipt, I could have gotten my money back.

10. Willy (brang, brought) his volleyball to the picnic.

11. I would have (become, became) very angry if you had not intervened.

12. I was exhausted because I had (swam, swum) two lengths of the pool.

13. Albert (eat, ate) four slices of almond fudge cake before he got sick.

14. How long has your watch been (broke, broken)?

15. If we had (knew, known) how the weather would be, we would not have gone on the trip.

16. The children had (did, done) the dishes as a surprise for their mother.

17. Teresa has (rode, ridden) all over the city looking for an apartment.

18. The burglar (ran, run) like a scared rabbit when he heard the alarm.

19. Someone had (took, taken) the wrong coat from the restaurant rack.

20. The trucker (drived, drove) all night; his eyes looked like poached eggs.

NAME: _____

DATE: _____

MASTERY TEST 2 | Irregular Verbs

Cross out the incorrect verb form. Write the correct form in the space provided.

_____ 1. The mop that I left by the door has froze stiff.

_____ 2. My car was stole, and I had no way of getting to school.

_____ 3. Someone leaved a book in the classroom.

_____ 4. Our gym teacher speaked on physical fitness, but we slept through the lecture.

_____ 5. That sweater was tore yesterday.

_____ 6. After I had loosed weight, the pants fit perfectly.

_____ 7. Ellen awaked from a sound sleep with the feeling there was someone in the house.

_____ 8. Life has dealed Lonnell a number of hard moments.

_____ 9. Father begun to yell at me as I walked in the door.

_____ 10. The sick puppy laid quietly on the veterinarian's table.

_____ 11. The instructor didn't remember that I had spoke to him.

_____ 12. While Alvin sung in the church choir, his mother beamed with pride and pleasure.

_____ 13. I would have went on vacation this week, but my boss asked me to wait a month.

_____ 14. When the boys throwed stones at us, we decided to throw some back.

_____ 15. I blowed up the balloon until it exploded in my face.

_____ 16. The body that the men taked out of the water was a terrible thing to see.

_____ 17. Rich breaked the Wii game that I lent him.

_____ 18. If the cell phone had rang once more, my mother would have tossed it in the garbage.

_____ 19. A sudden banging on the door shaked me out of sleep.

_____ 20. Granny has wore the same dress to every wedding and funeral for twenty years.

Number Correct

_____ x 10

_____ %

Irregular Verbs MASTERY TEST 3

Write in the space provided the correct form of the verb shown at the left.

sink   1. The fishing rod slipped out of his hand and _____ to the bottom of the pond.

choose   2. I _____ the blueberry pie for dessert because it looked delicious.

write   3. Pat had _____ the essay three times, but it still needed revision.

lie   4. As soon as I _____ down to take a nap, the phone rang.

catch   5. Greg _____ a cold while defrosting the refrigerator.

sell   6. The brothers worked on their old station wagon for a month and then _____ it for twice as much as they paid for it.

ride   7. Eric _____ the bucking bronco for a full thirty seconds before he was tossed into the sawdust.

hide   8. How did my little brother ever guess where his Christmas present was _____?

speak   9. If I _____ only when I was spoken to, I'd never get a word in edgewise.

shake   10. Susie's hands _____ as she handed in her paper.

Copyright © 2011 The McGraw-Hill Companies, Inc. All rights reserved.

169

NAME: _____

DATE: _____

MASTERY TEST 4   Irregular Verbs

Write in the space provided the correct form of the verb shown at the left.

ring   1. Sometimes the doorbell has _____ for several minutes before my grand-father notices the sounds.

shrink   2. My brand-new jeans _____ three sizes in the wash.

lend   3. Stella _____ someone her notebook and then forgot who had borrowed it.

rise   4. If taxes had not _____ so much this year, I could have afforded a vacation.

sleep   5. I turned in my term paper and then _____ for ten hours.

sting   6. Kim didn't see the bee in her sleeve and was _____ the moment she put her jacket on.

wear   7. Nick jogs five miles a day and has _____ out three pairs of running shoes this year.

burst   8. Cindy blew the biggest bubble I have ever seen. Then it _____, leaving shreds of pink bubble gum all over her face.

keep   9. I should have _____ my old coat instead of contributing it to the church rummage sale.

drive   10. We _____ for fifteen miles without seeing a single McDonald's.

Subject-Verb Agreement

Introductory Activity

As you read each pair of sentences below, write a check mark beside the sentence that you think uses the underlined word correctly.

The results of the election is very surprising. ___
The results of the election are very surprising. ___

There was many complaints about the violent TV show. ___
There were many complaints about the violent TV show. ___

Everybody usually gather at the waterfront on the Fourth of July. ___
Everybody usually gathers at the waterfront on the Fourth of July. ___

On the basis of the examples above, see if you can complete the following statements.

1. In the first two pairs of sentences, the subjects are _____ and

   _____. Since both these subjects are plural, the verb must be plural.

2. In the last pair of sentences, the subject, *Everybody,* is a word that

   is always (singular, plural), and so its accompanying verb must be

   (singular, plural).

Answers are on page 563.

A verb must agree with its subject in number. A *singular subject* (one person or thing) takes a singular verb. A *plural subject* (more than one person or thing) takes a plural verb. Mistakes in subject-verb agreement are sometimes made in the following situations:

1. When words come between the subject and the verb
2. When a verb comes before the subject
3. With indefinite pronouns
4. With compound subjects
5. With *who*, *which*, and *that*

Each situation is explained on the following pages.

Words between the Subject and the Verb

Words that come between the subject and the verb do not change subject-verb agreement.

The breakfast cereals in the pantry are made mostly of sugar.

In the example above, the subject (*cereals*) is plural and so the verb (*are*) is plural. The words *in the pantry* that come between the subject and the verb do not affect subject-verb agreement. To help find the subject of certain sentences, you should cross out prepositional phrases (explained on page 70):

One ~~of the crooked politicians~~ was jailed for a month.

The posters ~~on my little brother's wall~~ include hip-hop stars, athletes, and models in bathing suits.

Following is a list of common prepositions.

Common Prepositions				
about	before	by	inside	over
above	behind	during	into	through
across	below	except	of	to
among	beneath	for	off	toward
around	beside	from	on	under
at	between	in	onto	with

Draw one line under the subject. Then lightly cross out any words that come between the subject and the verb. Finally, draw two lines under the correct verb in parentheses.

Practice 1

EXAMPLE

The price of the stereo speakers (is, are) too high for my wallet.

1. The blue stain on the sheets (comes, come) from the cheap dish towel that I put in the washer with them.

2. The sport coat, along with the two pairs of pants, (sells, sell) for just fifty dollars.

3. The roots of the apple tree (is, are) very shallow.

4. Amir's sisters, who wanted to be at his surprise party, (was, were) unable to come because of flooded roads.

5. The dust-covered photo albums in the attic (belongs, belong) to my grandmother.

6. The cost of personal calls made on office telephones (is, are) deducted from our pay.

7. Two cups of coffee in the morning (does, do) not make up a hearty breakfast.

8. The moon as well as some stars (is, are) shining brightly tonight.

9. The electrical wiring in the apartment (is, are) dangerous and needs replacing.

10. Chapter 4 of the psychology book, along with six weeks of class notes, (is, are) to be the basis of the test.

Verb before the Subject

A verb agrees with its subject even when the verb comes *before* the subject. Words that may precede the subject include *there, here,* and, in questions, *who, which, what,* and *where.*

Inside the storage shed are the garden tools.

At the street corner were two panhandlers.

There are times I'm ready to quit my job.

Where are the instructions for the iPod?

> **TIP** If you are unsure about the subject, ask *who* or *what* of the verb. With the first sentence above, you might ask, "What are inside the storage shed?" The answer, garden *tools,* is the subject.

Practice

2

Underline the subject in each sentence. Then double-underline the correct verb in parentheses.

1. There (is, are) long lines at the checkout counter.

2. Scampering to the door to greet Martha Grencher (was, were) her two little dogs.

3. Filling the forest floor (was, were) dozens of pine cones.

4. There (is, are) pretzels if you want something to go with the cheese.

5. At the end of the line, hoping to get seats for the movie, (was, were) Janet and Maureen.

6. There (is, are) rats nesting under the backyard woodpile.

7. Swaggering down the street (was, were) several tough-looking boys.

8. On the very top of that mountain (is, are) a house for sale.

9. At the soap opera convention, there (was, were) fans from all over the country.

10. Under a large plastic dome on the side of the counter (lies, lie) a single gooey pastry.

Indefinite Pronouns

The following words, known as *indefinite pronouns,* always take singular verbs.

Indefinite Pronouns			
(-*one* words)	(-*body* words)	(-*thing* words)	
one	nobody	nothing	each
anyone	anybody	anything	either
everyone	everybody	everything	neither
someone	somebody	something	

TIP *Both* always takes a plural verb.

Write the correct form of the verb in the space provided.

hope, hopes   1. Everyone in our neighborhood _____ the farm stays open.

dances, dance   2. Nobody _____ the way he does.

deserves, deserve   3. Either of our football team's guards _____ to be an all-state guard.

was, were   4. Both of the race drivers _____ injured.

appears, appear   5. Everyone who received an invitation _____ to be here.

offers, offer   6. No one ever _____ to work on that committee.

owns, own   7. One of my sisters _____ a VW convertible.

has, have   8. Somebody _____ been taking shopping carts from the supermarket.

thinks, think   9. Everyone that I talked to _____ the curfew is a good idea.

has, have   10. Each of the candidates _____ talked about withdrawing from the race.

Compound Subjects

Subjects joined by *and* generally take a plural verb.

> <u>Yoga</u> and <u>biking</u> <u>are</u> Lola's ways of staying in shape.

> <u>Ambition</u> and <u>good luck</u> <u>are</u> the keys to his success.

When subjects are joined by *or, either… or, neither… nor, not only… but also,* the verb agrees with the subject closer to the verb.

> Either the restaurant <u>manager</u> or his <u>assistants</u> <u>deserve</u> to be fired for the spoiled meat used in the stew.

The nearer subject, *assistants*, is plural, and so the verb is plural.

Write the correct form of the verb in the space provided.

matches, match   1. This tie and shirt _____ the suit, but the shoes look terrible.

has, have   2. The kitchen and the bathroom _____ to be cleaned.

is, are   3. A good starting salary and a bonus system _____ the most attractive features of my new job.

plan, plans   4. Neither Ellen nor her brothers _____ to work at a temporary job during their holiday break from college.

is, are   5. For better or worse, working on his van and playing video games _____ Pete's main interests in life.

www.mhhe.com/langan

Who, Which, and That

When *who*, *which*, and *that* are used as subjects, they take singular verbs if the word they stand for is singular and plural verbs if the word they stand for is plural. For example, in the sentence

Gary is one of those people who are very private.

the verb is plural because *who* stands for *people*, which is plural. On the other hand, in the sentence

Gary is a person who is very private.

the verb is singular because *who* stands for *person*, which is singular.

Practice 5

Write the correct form of the verb in the space provided.

was, were   1. I removed the sheets that _____ jamming my washer.

stumbles, stumble   2. This job isn't for people who _____ over tough decisions.

blares, blare   3. The radio that _____ all night belongs to my insomniac neighbor.

gives, give   4. The Saturn is one of the small American cars that _____ high gasoline mileage.

appears, appear   5. The strange smell that _____ in our neighborhood on rainy days is being investigated.

Collaborative Activity

Editing and Rewriting

Working with a partner, read the short paragraph below and mark off the five mistakes in subject-verb agreement. Then use the space provided to correct the five agreement errors. Feel free to discuss the rewrite quietly with your partner and refer back to the chapter when necessary.

When most people think about cities, they do not thinks about wild animals. But in my city apartment, there is enough creatures to fill a small forest. In the daytime, I must contend with the pigeons. These unwanted guests of my apartment makes a loud feathery mess on my bedroom windowsill. In the evening, my apartment is visited by roaches. These large insects creep onto my kitchen floor and walls after dark and

NAME: _____

DATE: _____

Subject-Verb Agreement MASTERY TEST 5

Underline the correct verb in the parentheses. Note that you will first have to determine the subject in each sentence. To help find subjects in certain sentences, you may find it helpful to cross out prepositional phrases.

1. All the animals for sale in that pet store (looks, look) unhealthy.

2. The extra fees on my new cell phone bill (is, are) too high.

3. One of my instructors (has, have) a hybrid car.

4. Wet roads and dangerous driving (was, were) to blame for the accident.

5. Not one cash register in the store (is, are) working correctly.

6. Once a year, Jim and his buddies (goes, go) fishing.

7. The books in the library (was, were) damaged by the flood.

8. Crawling across the kitchen floor (was, were) three hairy spiders.

9. The employees of the hospital (wants, want) a pay raise.

10. Neither Kevin nor Denise (wants, want) to talk about their relationship.

11. A stack of folded shirts in the Laundromat (was, were) stolen.

12. Someone once said, "Politics (is, are) a dirty business."

13. A few kids on the high school team (hopes, hope) to play college football.

14. Hakeem is one of those guys who (knows, know) how to fix anything.

15. The buttons on the old keyboard (is, are) dirty from use.

16. The executives of that company (makes, make) ten times as much as any of their employees.

17. The old houses across the street on our block (needs, need) major repairs.

18. Shoppers in the long line at the closeout sale in the mall (was, were) muttering angrily to themselves.

19. Physics (is, are) a subject that requires strong math skills.

20. The chrome wheels on the classic Ford Mustang (shines, shine).

SECTION 2
Verbs, Pronouns, and Agreement

11

Consistent Verb Tense

Introductory Activity

See if you can find and underline the two mistakes in verb tense in the following selection.

When Computer Warehouse had a sale, Alex decided to buy a new personal computer. He planned to set up the machine himself and hoped to connect it to the Internet right away. When he arrived home, however, Alex discovers that hooking up the wires to the computer could be complicated and confusing. The directions sounded as if they had been written for electrical engineers. After two hours of frustration, Alex gave up and calls a technician for help.

Now try to complete the following statement:

Verb tenses should be consistent. In the selection above, two verbs have to be changed because they are mistakenly in the (*present, past*) _____ tense while all the other verbs in the selection are in the (*present, past*) _____ tense.

Answers are on page 564.

Keeping Tenses Consistent

Do not shift tenses unnecessarily. If you begin writing a paper in the present tense, don't shift suddenly to the past. If you begin in the past, don't shift without reason to the present. Notice the inconsistent verb tenses in the following example:

> Smoke <u>spilled</u> from the front of the overheated car. The driver <u>opens</u> up the hood, then <u>jumped</u> back as steam <u>billows</u> out.

The verbs must be consistently in the present tense:

> Smoke <u>spills</u> from the front of the overheated car. The driver <u>opens</u> up the hood, then <u>jumps</u> back as steam <u>billows</u> out.

Or the verbs must be consistently in the past tense:

> Smoke <u>spilled</u> from the front of the overheated car. The driver <u>opened</u> up the hood, then <u>jumped</u> back as steam <u>billowed</u> out.

www.mhhe.com/langan

In each item, one verb must be changed so that it agrees in tense with the other verbs. Cross out the incorrect verb and write the correct form in the space at the left.

Practice

1

EXAMPLE

<u>looked</u>   I gave away my striped sweater after three people told me I ~~look~~ like a giant bee.

_____   1. Mike peels and eats oranges at movies; the smell caused other people to move away from him.

_____   2. The nursing program attracted Juanita, but she weighed the pluses and minuses and then decides to enroll in the x-ray technician course instead.

_____   3. I grabbed for the last bag of pretzels on the supermarket shelf. But when I pick it up, I discovered there was a tear in the cellophane bag.

_____   4. Roger waits eagerly for the mail carrier each day. Part of him hoped to get a letter in which someone declares she is madly in love with him and will cherish him forever.

_____   5. The first thing Jerry does every day is weigh himself. The scale informed him what he can eat that day.

_____   6. My sister sprinkles detergent flakes on my head and then ran around telling everyone that I had dandruff.

_____   7. When Norm peeled back the old shingles, he discovers that the roof was rotted through.

_____ 8. My father knocked on the bedroom door. When he asks me if he could come in, I said, "Not right now."

_____ 9. Omar is so unaggressive that when a clerk overcharged him for an item, he pays the money and makes no comment.

_____ 10. When my doctor told me I needed an operation, I swallow hard and my stomach churned.

Review Test   1

Change the verbs where needed in the following selection so that they are consistently in the past tense. Cross out each incorrect verb and write the correct form above it, as shown in the example. You will need to make nine corrections.

¹Last week, I began driving to work, as usual. ²I drove up the expressway ramp and *merged* merge into three lanes of speeding cars. ³I turned on the radio and settle in for another twenty-five minutes of tension and pressure. ⁴Then, about five miles on, I saw something unusual. ⁵Up ahead, stranded on the narrow concrete island that separated three lanes of eastbound traffic from three lanes of westbound traffic, was a small brown dog. ⁶Streams of zooming cars pass the animal like two rushing rivers. ⁷Several times, the dog attempt to cross the road. ⁸He moves gingerly onto the highway, only to jump back at the approach of a car. ⁹I realize it was only a matter of time before the panicky dog bolt into the traffic and kill itself. ¹⁰I didn't know what to do. ¹¹I slow my car down a little and wondered if I should pull onto the shoulder. ¹²Then, I heard a welcome sound—a police siren. ¹³Someone must have called the state police about the dog. ¹⁴In my rearview mirror, I saw the patrol car and a white van labeled "Animal Control." ¹⁵I drove on, confident that the dog would be rescued and relieve that someone had cared enough to save its small life.

Tenses	Examples
Present	I *work*. Tanya *works*.
Past	Howard *worked* on the lawn.
Future	You *will work* overtime this week.
Present perfect	Gail *has worked* hard on the puzzle. They *have worked* well together.
Past perfect	They *had worked* eight hours before their shift ended.
Future perfect	The volunteers *will have worked* many unpaid hours.
Present progressive	I *am* not *working* today. You *are working* the second shift. The clothes dryer *is* not *working* properly.
Past progressive	She *was working* outside. The plumbers *were working* here this morning.
Future progressive	The sound system *will be working* by tonight.
Present perfect progressive	Married life *has* not *been working* out for that couple.
Past perfect progressive	I *had been working* overtime until recently.
Future perfect progressive	My sister *will have been working* at that store for eleven straight months by the time she takes a vacation next week.

www.mhhe.com/langan

The perfect tenses are formed by adding *have, has,* or *had* to the past participle (the form of the verb that ends, usually, in *-ed*). The progressive tenses are formed by adding *am, is, are, was,* or *were* to the present participle (the form of the verb that ends in *-ing*). The perfect progressive tenses are formed by adding *have been, has been,* or *had been* to the present participle.

Certain tenses are explained in more detail on the following pages.

Present Perfect
(*have* or *has* + past participle)

The present perfect tense expresses an action that began in the past and has recently been completed or is continuing in the present.

The city *has* just *agreed* on a contract with the sanitation workers.

Tony's parents *have lived* in that house for twenty years.

Sarah *has enjoyed* vampire novels since she was a little girl.

Past Perfect
(*had* + past participle)

The past perfect tense expresses a past action that was completed before another past action.

Lola *had learned* to dance by the time she was five.

The class *had* just *started* when the fire bell rang.

Bad weather *had* never *been* a problem on our vacations until last year.

Present Progressive
(*am, is,* or *are* + -*ing* form)

The present progressive tense expresses an action still in progress.

I *am taking* an early train into the city every day this week.

Karl *is playing* softball over at the field.

The vegetables *are growing* rapidly.

Past Progressive
(*was* or *were* + -*ing* form)

The past progressive expresses an action that was in progress in the past.

I *was spending* several hours a day following celebrities on Twitter before I got bored and started writing songs.

Last week, the store *was selling* many items at half price.

My friends *were driving* over to pick me up when the accident occurred.

Practice

1

For the sentences that follow, fill in the present or past perfect or the present or past progressive of the verb shown. Use the tense that seems to express the meaning of each sentence best.

EXAMPLE

park   This summer, Mickey ____*is parking*____ cars at a French restaurant.

walk   1. We _____ for five miles before we realized we were lost.

feel   2. The new mail carrier _____ good about his job until the first dog bit him.

place   3. After an hour, the waiter _____ only a basket of stale rolls on our table.

try   4. All last winter, my little brother _____ to teach himself to build a Web site.

grow   5. This year, Aunt Agatha _____ tomatoes—she must have about five hundred already.

look   6. I _____ everywhere for the paper; finally, I found it under the cat.

study   7. Miriam _____ French for three years so she can talk to her poodle.

see   8. James loves karate; he _____ every Bruce Lee movie in existence.

watch   9. Nilsa _____ soap operas for four hours a day during the two months she was unemployed.

throw   10. The pitcher _____ to second; unfortunately, the runner was on third.

Verbals

Verbals are words formed from verbs. Verbals, like verbs, often express action. They can add variety to your sentences and vigor to your writing style. The three kinds of verbals are *infinitives, participles,* and *gerunds*.

www.mhhe.com/langan

Infinitive

An infinitive is *to* plus the base form of the verb.

> I started *to practice.*
> Don't try *to lift* that table.
> I asked Russ *to drive* me home.

Participle

A participle is a verb form used as an adjective (a descriptive word). The present participle ends in *-ing*. The past participle ends in *-ed* or has an irregular ending.

> *Favoring* his *cramped* leg, the *screaming* boy waded out of the pool.
>
> The *laughing* child held up her *locked* piggy bank.
>
> *Using* a shovel and a bucket, I scooped water out of the *flooded* basement.

Gerund

A gerund is the *-ing* form of a verb used as a noun.

> *Studying* wears me out.
>
> *Playing* basketball is my main pleasure during the week.
>
> Through *jogging*, you can get yourself in shape.

Practice 2

In the space beside each sentence, identify the italicized word as a participle (*P*), an infinitive (*I*), or a gerund (*G*).

_____ 1. The *sobbing* child could not find his parents.

_____ 2. *Gossiping* with neighbors is my favorite pastime.

_____ 3. *Painting* the front porch is a chore Fred promises to get to every spring.

_____ 4. All my brother ever wants *to do* is download new apps on his iPhone.

_____ 5. Lola always liked *to race* through a pile of dead leaves.

_____ 6. My boss's *graying* hair gives him a look of authority.

_____ 7. *Glowing* embers were all that remained of the fire.

_____ 8. It doesn't matter if you win or lose—just try *to break* even.

_____ 9. *Holding* her nose, my mother asked, "What's that awful smell?"

_____ 10. *Wearing* glasses makes that man look intelligent.

Active and Passive Verbs

www.mhhe.com/langan

When the subject of a sentence performs the action of a verb, the verb is in the *active voice*. When the subject of a sentence receives the action of a verb, the verb is in the *passive voice*.

The passive form of a verb consists of a form of the verb *be* plus the past participle of the main verb. Look at the active and passive forms of the verbs below.

Active	Passive
Lola *ate* the vanilla pudding. (The subject, *Lola*, is the doer of the action.)	The vanilla pudding *was eaten by* Lola. (The subject, *pudding*, does not act. Instead, something happens to it.)
The plumber *replaced* the water heater. (The subject, *plumber,* is the doer of the action.)	The water heater *was replaced by* the plumber. (The subject, *heater,* does not act. Instead, something happens to it.)

In general, active verbs are more effective than passive ones. Active verbs give your writing a simpler and more vigorous style. The passive form of verbs is appropriate, however, when the performer of the action is unknown or is less important than the receiver of the action. For example:

My house was vandalized last night.
(The performer of the action is unknown.)

Troy was seriously injured as a result of your negligence.
(The receiver of the action, *Troy,* is being emphasized.)

Change the following sentences from the passive to the active voice. Note that you may have to add a subject in some cases.

Practice 3

EXAMPLE

The Vespa was ridden by Tony.
Tony rode the Vespa.

The basketball team was given a standing ovation.
The crowd gave the basketball team a standing ovation.

(Here a subject had to be added.)

1. The surprise party was organized by Eliza.

   _____

2. Many people were offended by the comedian.

   _____

3. The old woman's groceries are paid for by the neighbors.

   _____

4. The horse chestnuts were knocked off the trees by the boys.

_____

5. The devil was driven out of Regan by the exorcist.

_____

6. The huge moving van was loaded by four perspiring men.

_____

7. A tray of glasses was dropped by the inexperienced waiter.

_____

8. Umbrellas are always being lost by my forgetful Aunt Agatha.

_____

9. Babe Ruth's home run record was finally broken by Barry Bonds.

_____

10. A bomb was found in the suitcase by the airport security staff.

_____

Review Test   1

On separate paper, write three sentences apiece that use:

1. Present perfect tense

2. Past perfect tense

3. Present progressive tense

4. Past progressive tense

5. Infinitive

6. Participle

7. Gerund

8. Passive voice (when the subject is unknown or is less important than the receiver of an action—see pages 196–197)

Unclear	Clear
Maggie told Masako that her guitar playing had improved.	Maggie told Masako, "Your guitar playing has improved."
(*Who* had improved: Maggie or Masako? Be clear.)	(Quotation marks, which can sometimes be used to correct an unclear reference, are explained in Chapter 25.)
My older brother is an electrician, but I'm not interested in it.	My older brother is an electrician, but I'm not interested in becoming one.
(There is no specific word that *it* refers to. It would not make sense to say, "I'm not interested in electrician.")	
Our instructor did not explain the assignment, which made me angry.	I was angry that our instructor did not explain the assignment.
(Does *which* mean that the instructor's failure to explain the assignment made you angry or that the assignment itself made you angry? Be clear.)	

Rewrite each of the following sentences to make clear the vague pronoun reference. Add, change, or omit words as necessary.

Practice

1

EXAMPLE

Lana thanked Rita for the gift, which was very thoughtful of her.

Lana thanked Rita for the thoughtful gift.

1. Mario insisted to Harry that it was his turn to drive.

_____

_____

2. I failed two of my courses last semester because they graded unfairly.

_____

_____

3. Don was offered an accounting job, which pleased his parents very much.

_____

_____

4. When Tony questioned the mechanic, he became very upset.

_____

_____

5. I was very nervous about the biology exam, which was unexpected.

_____

_____

6. Paul told his younger brother that the dog had chewed his new running shoes.

_____

_____

7. My cousin is an astrologer, but I don't believe in it.

_____

_____

8. Liz told Elaine that she had been promoted.

_____

_____

9. Whenever I start enjoying a new television show, they take it off the air.

_____

_____

10. When the center fielder heard the crack of the bat, he raced toward the fence but was unable to catch it.

_____

_____

www.mhhe.com/langan

Pronoun Agreement

A pronoun must agree in number with the word or words it replaces. If the word a pronoun refers to is singular, the pronoun must be singular; if the word is plural, the pronoun must be plural. (Note that the word a pronoun refers to is known as the *antecedent.*)

Lola agreed to lend me her Billie Holiday CDs.

The gravediggers sipped coffee during their break.

In the first example, the pronoun *her* refers to the singular word *Lola;* in the second example, the pronoun *their* refers to the plural word *gravediggers.*

Write the appropriate pronoun (*they, their, them, it*) in the blank space in each of the following sentences.

Practice 2

EXAMPLE

My credit cards got me into debt, so I burned _____*them*_____.

1. After the hikers arrived at the camp, _____ removed _____ heavy packs.

2. That breakfast cereal is delicious, but _____ has almost no nutrients.

3. I never buy gifts in stores anymore, for I use my computer to purchase _____ on the Internet.

4. The heat was so oppressive during the race that _____ caused several runners to pass out.

5. Anna's parents went to a marriage counselor, and _____ are getting along better now.

www.mhhe.com/langan

Indefinite Pronouns

The following words, known as *indefinite pronouns,* are always singular.

Indefinite Pronouns		
(*-one* words)	(*-body* words)	
one	nobody	each
anyone	anybody	either
everyone	everybody	neither
someone	somebody	

Either of the apartments has its drawbacks.

One of the girls lost her skateboard.

Everyone in the class must hand in his paper tomorrow.

In each example, the pronoun is singular because it refers to one of the indefinite pronouns. There are two important points to remember about indefinite pronouns.

Point 1 The last example above suggests that everyone in the class is male. If the students were all female, the pronoun would be *her*. If the students were a mixed group of males and females, the pronoun form would be *his or her*.

Everyone in the class must hand in *his or her* paper tomorrow.

Some writers still follow the traditional practice of using *his* to refer to both men and women. Many now use *his or her* to avoid an implied sexual bias. Perhaps the best practice, though, is to avoid using either *his* or the somewhat awkward *his or her*. This can often be done by rewriting a sentence in the plural:

All students in the class must hand in *their* papers tomorrow.

Here are some examples of sentences that can be rewritten in the plural.

A young child is seldom willing to share her toys with others.
Young children are seldom willing to share their toys with others.

Anyone who does not wear his seat belt will be fined.
People who do not wear their seat belts will be fined.

A newly elected politician should not forget his or her campaign promises.
Newly elected politicians should not forget their campaign promises.

Point 2 In informal spoken English, *plural* pronouns are often used with indefinite pronouns. Instead of saying

Everybody has *his or her* own idea of an ideal vacation.

we are likely to say

Everybody has *their* own idea of an ideal vacation.

Here are other examples:

Everyone in the class must pass in *their* papers.
Everybody in our club has *their* own idea about how to raise money.
No one in our family skips *their* chores.

Possessive pronouns show ownership or possession.

> Clyde revved up *his* motorcycle and blasted off.
> The keys are *mine.*

Points to Remember about Possessive Pronouns

Point 1

A possessive pronoun *never* uses an apostrophe. (See also page 326.)

Incorrect	Correct
That coat is *hers'.*	That coat is *hers.*
The card table is *theirs'.*	The card table is *theirs.*

Point 2

Do not use any of the following nonstandard forms to show possession.

Incorrect	Correct
I met a friend of *him.*	I met a friend of *his.*
Can I use *you* car?	Can I use *your* car?
Me sister is in the hospital.	*My* sister is in the hospital.
That magazine is *mines.*	That magazine is *mine.*

Cross out the incorrect pronoun form in each of the sentences that follow. Write the correct form in the space at the left.

Practice

5

EXAMPLE

___My___   ~~Me~~ car has broken down again.

_____ 1. That car won't be safe until you get its' brakes fixed.

_____ 2. If you are a friend of him, you're welcome to stay with us.

_____ 3. The seat you are sitting on is mines.

_____ 4. The neighbors called they dogs to chase the cat off the lawn.

_____ 5. The coffeepot is ours'.

Demonstrative Pronouns

Demonstrative pronouns point to or single out a person or thing. There are four demonstrative pronouns:

Demonstrative Pronouns

this	these
that	those

Generally speaking, *this* and *these* refer to things close at hand; *that* and *those* refer to things farther away.

Is anyone using *this* spoon?

I am going to throw away *these* magazines.

I just bought *that* silver Honda at the curb.

Pick up *those* toys in the corner.

TIP Do not use *them, this here, that there, these here,* or *those there* to point out. Use only *this, that, these,* or *those.*

Incorrect	Correct
Them tires are badly worn.	*Those* tires are badly worn.
This here book looks hard to read.	*This* book looks hard to read.
That there candy is delicious.	*That* candy is delicious.
Those there squirrels are pests.	*Those* squirrels are pests.

Practice

6

Cross out the incorrect form of the demonstrative pronoun and write the correct form in the space provided.

EXAMPLE

Those   ~~Them~~ clothes need washing.

_____ 1. That there dog will bite you if it gets a chance.

_____ 2. This here fingernail is not growing straight.

_____ 3. Them girls cannot be trusted.

_____ 4. Carry in those there shopping bags if you want to help.

_____ 5. The place where I'd like to live is that there corner house.

Look at the photo above and write four sentences about it using *this, that, these,* and *those.*

Practice

7

_____

_____

_____

_____

Reflexive Pronouns

Reflexive pronouns are pronouns that refer to the subject of a sentence. Here is a list of reflexive pronouns.

Reflexive Pronouns		
myself	herself	ourselves
yourself	itself	yourselves
himself		themselves

Sometimes the reflexive pronoun is used for emphasis:

You will have to wash the dishes *yourself.*

We *ourselves* are willing to forget the matter.

The president *himself* turns down his living room thermostat.

Points to Remember about Reflexive Pronouns

Point 1

In the plural *-self* becomes *-selves.*

> Lola washes *herself* in lavender bath oil.
>
> They treated *themselves* to a Bermuda vacation.

Point 2

Be careful that you do not use any of the following incorrect forms as reflexive pronouns.

Incorrect	Correct
He believes in *hisself.*	He believes in *himself.*
We drove the children *ourself.*	We drove the children *ourselves.*
They saw *themself* in the fun house mirror.	They saw *themselves* in the fun house mirror.
I'll do it *meself.*	I'll do it *myself.*

Practice

8

Cross out the incorrect form of the reflexive pronoun and write the correct form in the space at the left.

EXAMPLE

themselves   She believes that God helps those who help ~~themself~~.

_____ 1. Tony considers hisself the strongest wrestler in the class.

_____ 2. The striking players are only making theirselves look greedy.

_____ 3. You must carry your luggage yourselfs.

_____ 4. Many firefighters themself do not have smoke detectors in their homes.

_____ 5. We decided to finish the basement by ourself.

Review Test   1

Underline the correct word in the parentheses.

1. I'm going to leave if (that, that there) waiter doesn't come over here soon.

2. Though secured by a chain, the snarling German shepherd still terrified Lee and (I, me).

3. That iPod is (mine, mines).

4. Watching Alan and (I, me) dancing made him grit his teeth.

5. My aunts promised (us, we) girls a trip to Italy for graduation.

6. The service manager did not remember (who, whom) worked on my car.

7. I think (those, those there) people should be kicked out of the theater for talking.

8. The giggling boys only made (themself, themselves) look foolish.

9. If the decision were up to (they, them), my position in the company would be that of full-time pencil sharpener.

10. If (she, her) and Sandy had reported the leak, the cellar would not have flooded.

Review Test 2

Cross out the pronoun error in each sentence and write the correct form above it.

EXAMPLE

Terry and *me* have already seen the movie. [*I* written above *me*]

1. Our friends have gotten theirselves into debt by overusing credit cards.

2. This here heat pump will lower your energy bill.

3. Watching the football game, us fans soon realized that our team would lose.

4. If you and her get confused about directions, stop and check at a service station.

5. Dimitri felt both sorry for and angry at the drug addict whom tried to steal his car.

6. Before he took a foul shot, the basketball player crossed hisself for good luck.

7. Jane and me refused to join the union.

8. The parents theirselfs must share the blame for their child's failure in school.

9. Our class painted more colorful posters than them.

10. You and me have got to have a talk.

Review Test 3

On separate paper, write sentences that use correctly each of the following words or word groups.

EXAMPLE

Peter and him *The coach suspended Peter and him.*

1. those

2. Sue and she

3. faster than I

4. ours

5. Lola and me

6. whom

7. yourselves

8. with Linda and him

9. you and I

10. the neighbors and us

NAME: _____

DATE: _____

Pronoun Types **MASTERY TEST 1**

Underline the correct word in parentheses.

1. Harold pretended to be at ease, but he didn't fool Susan or (me, I).

2. (This, This here) tree is full of sparrows at night.

3. I believe that coat is (hers', hers).

4. Talking intimately, Zoe and (I, me) didn't see Earl walking up to our front porch.

5. The two of you must give (yourself, yourselves) another chance.

6. Al and (I, me) are equally poor in math.

7. My car's front tires, (who, which) vibrate at high speeds, need to be realigned.

8. (Those, Them) newspapers have to be carried down to the incinerator.

9. That last hamburger on the grill is (yours', yours) if you want it.

10. Though the furry black tarantula was in a cage, it still scared Manuel and (I, me).

11. Whenever our neighbor sees me on the porch, he invites (hisself, himself) over.

12. You are getting more work done than (I, me).

13. Ted (hisself, himself) takes full responsibility for the accident.

14. The instructor glared at Sarah and (I, me) and then dismissed the class.

15. Though younger than (I, me), Andrea acts like my superior.

16. When I miss class, I get together later with a student (who, whom) takes good notes.

17. Of all the children in the class, Dora and (he, him) are the least reliable.

18. The professor asked Chico and (I, me) to volunteer.

19. I recently met a friend of (her, hers).

20. (Those, Them) boots weren't made for walking.

NAME: _____

DATE: _____

MASTERY TEST 2 | ## Pronoun Types

Cross out the incorrect pronoun in each sentence and write the correct form in the space provided at the left.

_____ 1. The coach's decision didn't suit Charlie or I.

_____ 2. Our instructor gave us homework in all of those there books.

_____ 3 That rabbit of yours' just became a mother again.

_____ 4. Joel won because he has played chess much longer than her.

_____ 5. Our brothers were very proud of themself when they caught the vandal in our neighborhood.

_____ 6. The women whom filed the class action suit were initially fired by the company.

_____ 7. The mail carrier says that Tyrell and me get more mail than all the other people on the block combined.

_____ 8. Lee never gets tired of talking about hisself.

_____ 9. Even the United States mail gets things done faster than her.

_____ 10. This here toothbrush looks as if someone used it to scrub potatoes.

_____ 11. Angela and me go hiking together each fall.

_____ 12. The firefighters theirselfs were puzzled by the source of the smoke in my basement.

_____ 13. Our garden is better cared for than theirs'.

_____ 14. The stone barely missed we and the children.

_____ 15. Them mosquitoes will bite you faster than you can blink your eyes.

_____ 16. If you want that old garden shovel, it's yours'.

_____ 17. I heard that her and her sister were expelled from school.

_____ 18. Julio is looking for someone to who he can sell his car.

_____ 19. Pete jogs on a more regular basis than me.

_____ 20. The pages are torn in many of them books.

Adjectives and Adverbs

15

Introductory Activity

Write in an appropriate word or words to complete each of the sentences below.

1. The teenage years were a _____ time for me.
2. The mechanic listened _____ while I described my car problem.
3. Basketball is a _____ game than football.
4. My brother is the _____ person in our family.

Now see if you can complete the following sentences.

The word inserted in the first sentence is an (adjective, adverb); it describes the word *time*.

The word inserted in the second sentence is an (adjective, adverb); it probably ends in the two letters _____ and describes the word *listened*.

The word inserted in the third sentence is a comparative adjective; it may be preceded by *more* or end in the two letters _____.

The word inserted in the fourth sentence is a superlative adjective; it may be preceded by *most* or end in the three letters _____.

Answers are on page 566.

Adjectives and adverbs are descriptive words. Their purpose is to make the meaning of the words they describe more specific.

Adjectives

What Are Adjectives?

Adjectives describe nouns (names of persons, places, or things) or pronouns.

> Charlotte is a *kind* woman. (The adjective *kind* describes the noun *woman*.)
>
> He is *tired*. (The adjective *tired* describes the pronoun *he*.)

An adjective usually comes before the word it describes (as in *kind woman*). But it can also come after forms of the verb *be (is, are, was, were,* and so on). Less often, an adjective follows verbs such as *feel, look, smell, sound, taste, appear, become,* and *seem*.

> The bureau is *heavy.* (The adjective *heavy* describes the bureau.)
>
> These pants are *itchy. (*The adjective *itchy* describes the pants.)
>
> The children seem *restless.* (The adjective *restless* describes the children.)

What is your opinion of the above artwork? What thoughts and feelings come to mind as you view it? On a separate piece of paper, use adjectives to describe your feelings about this artwork. Write at least three sentences using adjectives.

www.mhhe.com/langan

Using Adjectives to Compare

For most short adjectives, add *-er* when comparing two things and *-est* when comparing three or more things.

> I am *taller* than my brother, but my father is the *tallest* person in the house.

> The farm market sells *fresher* vegetables than the corner store, but the *freshest* vegetables are the ones grown in my own garden.

For most *longer* adjectives (two or more syllables), add *more* when comparing two things and *most* when comparing three or more things.

> Backgammon is *more enjoyable* to me than checkers, but chess is the *most enjoyable* game of all.

> My mother is *more talkative* than my father, but my grandfather is the *most talkative* person in the house.

Points to Remember about Adjectives

Point 1

Be careful not to use both an *-er* ending and *more*, or both an *-est* ending and *most*.

Incorrect	Correct
Football is a *more livelier* game than baseball.	Football is a *livelier* game than baseball.
Tod Traynor was voted the *most likeliest* to succeed in our high school class.	Tod Traynor was voted the *most likely* to succeed in our high school class.

Point 2

Pay special attention to the following words, each of which has irregular forms.

	Comparative (Two)	Superlative (Three or More)
bad	worse	worst
good, well	better	best
little	less	least
much, many	more	most

Practice 1

Fill in the comparative or superlative forms for the following adjectives. Two are done for you as examples.

	Comparative (Two)	Superlative (Three or More)
fast	_faster_	_fastest_
timid	_more timid_	_most timid_
kind	_____	_____
ambitious	_____	_____
generous	_____	_____
fine	_____	_____
likable	_____	_____

Practice 2

Add to each sentence the correct form of the word in the margin.

EXAMPLE

bad   The _____worst_____ day of my life was the one when my house caught fire.

comfortable   1. My jeans are the _____ pants I own.

difficult   2. My biology exam was the _____ of my five exams.

easy   3. The _____ way to get a good grade in the class is to take effective notes.

little   4. I made _____ money in my job as a delivery boy than I made as a golf caddy.

good   5. The _____ pay I ever made was as a drill press operator in a machine shop.

long   6. The ticket lines for the rock concert were the _____ I had ever seen.

memorable   7. The _____ days of my childhood were the ones I spent on trips with my grandfather.

experienced   8. I am a _____ driver than my sister, but my brother is the _____ driver in the family.

What Dangling Modifiers Are and How to Correct Them

A modifier that opens a sentence must be followed immediately by the word it is meant to describe. Otherwise, the modifier is said to be *dangling,* and the sentence takes on an unintended meaning. For example, look at this sentence:

> While sleeping in his backyard, a Frisbee hit Bill on the head.

The unintended meaning is that the *Frisbee* was sleeping in his backyard. What the writer meant, of course, was that *Bill* was sleeping in his backyard. The writer should have placed *Bill* right after the modifier, revising the rest of the sentence as necessary:

> While sleeping in his backyard, *Bill* was hit on the head by a Frisbee.

www.mhhe.com/langan

The sentence could also be corrected by adding the missing subject and verb to the opening word group:

> While *Bill* was sleeping in his backyard, a Frisbee hit him on the head.

Other sentences with dangling modifiers follow. Read the explanations of why they are dangling, and look carefully at how they are corrected.

Dangling	Correct
Having almost no money, my survival depended on my parents.	Having almost no money, *I* depended on my parents for survival.
(*Who* has almost no money? The answer is not *survival* but *I.* The subject *I* must be added.)	*Or:* Since *I* had almost no money, I depended on my parents for survival.
Riding his bike, a German shepherd bit Tony on the ankle.	Riding his bike, *Tony* was bitten on the ankle by a German shepherd.
(*Who* is riding the bike? The answer is not *German shepherd,* as it unintentionally seems to be, but *Tony.* The subject *Tony* must be added.)	*Or:* While *Tony* was riding his bike, a German shepherd bit him on the ankle.
When trying to lose weight, all snacks are best avoided.	When trying to lose weight, *you* should *avoid* all snacks.
(*Who* is trying to lose weight? The answer is not *snacks* but *you.* The subject *you* must be added.)	*Or:* When *you* are trying to lose weight, *avoid* all snacks.

These examples make clear two ways of correcting a dangling modifier. Decide on a logical subject and do one of the following:

1. Place the subject *within* the opening word group:

Since *I* had almost no money, I depended on my parents for survival.

In some cases an appropriate subordinating word such as *since* must be added, and the verb may have to be changed slightly as well.

2. Place the subject right *after* the opening word group:

Having almost no money, *I* depended on my parents for survival.

Sometimes even more rewriting is necessary to correct a dangling modifier. What is important to remember is that a modifier must be placed as close as possible to the word that it modifies.

Practice

1

Rewrite each sentence to correct the dangling modifier. Mark the one sentence that is correct with a *C.*

1. Folded into a tiny square, I could not read the message.

   _____

   _____

2. Wading into the lake, tadpoles swirled around my ankles.

   _____

   _____

3. Soaked to the skin, Chris was miserable waiting in the unsheltered doorway.

   _____

   _____

4. Hanging on the wall, I saw a photograph of my mother.

   _____

   _____

5. Settling comfortably into the chair, the television captured my attention for the next hour.

   _____

   _____

Dangling Modifiers MASTERY TEST 2

Underline the dangling modifier in each sentence. Then rewrite the sentence, correcting the dangling modifier.

1. While cutting the lawn, five mosquitoes bit me.

   _____

   _____

2. Smoking in the rest room, my math teacher caught Fred and me.

   _____

   _____

3. Shortly before giving birth, the doctor gave his wife a sedative.

   _____

   _____

4. Quickly taking the sheets off the clothesline, rain pelted our faces.

   _____

   _____

5. Dripping with perspiration, the air-conditioned store offered us relief.

   _____

   _____

6. While shopping at the store, my bike was stolen.

   _____

   _____

7. Hurrying to class, my English paper fell out of my notebook into a puddle.

   _____

   _____

8. After watching two movies at the drive-in, my stomach began rumbling for pizza.

   _____

   _____

Faulty Parallelism

18

Introductory Activity

Read aloud each pair of sentences below. Write a check mark beside the sentence that reads more smoothly and clearly and sounds more natural.

Pair 1

_____ I use my computer for writing papers, surfing the Web, and to contact my friends on Facebook.

_____ I use my computer to write papers, to surf the Web, and to contact my friends on Facebook.

Pair 2

_____ One option Sonja had was to stay in the Air Force; the other was returning to college.

_____ One option Sonja had was to stay in the Air Force; the other was to return to college.

Pair 3

_____ Dad's favorite chair has a torn cushion, the armrest is stained, and a musty odor.

_____ Dad's favorite chair has a torn cushion, a stained armrest, and a musty odor.

Answers are on page 567.

Parallelism Explained

Words in a pair or a series should have parallel structure. By balancing the items in a pair or a series so that they have the same kind of structure, you will make the sentence clearer and easier to read. Notice how the parallel sentences that follow read more smoothly than the nonparallel ones.

www.mhhe.com/langan

Nonparallel (Not Balanced)

Fran spends her free time reading, listening to music, and she works in the garden.

After the camping trip I was exhausted, irritable, and wanted to eat.

My hope for retirement is to be healthy, to live in a comfortable house, and having plenty of money.

Nightly, Alexei puts out the trash, checks the locks on the doors, and the burglar alarm is turned on.

Parallel (Balanced)

Fran spends her free time reading, listening to music, and working in the garden.

(A balanced series of -ing words: *reading, listening, working.*)

After the camping trip I was exhausted, irritable, and hungry.

(A balanced series of descriptive words: *exhausted, irritable, hungry.*)

My hope for retirement is to be healthy, to live in a comfortable house, and to have plenty of money.

(A balanced series of *to* verbs: *to be, to live, to have.*)

Nightly, Alexei puts out the trash, checks the locks on the doors, and turns on the burglar alarm.

(Balanced verbs and word order: *puts out the trash, checks the locks, turns on the burglar alarm.*)

Balanced sentences are not a skill you need to worry about when you are writing first drafts. But when you rewrite, you should try to put matching words and ideas into matching structures. Such parallelism will improve your writing style.

The unbalanced part of each sentence is italicized. Rewrite this part so that it matches the rest of the sentence.

1   EXAMPLE

In the afternoon, I changed two diapers, ironed several shirts, and *was watching* soap operas. _watched_____

1. After the exercise class, I woke up with stiff knees, throbbing legs, and *arms that ached.* _____

2. Our favorite restaurant specializes in delicious omelets, *soups that are freshly made,* and inexpensive desserts. _____

3. The man running the checkout counter was tall, thin, and *having a bad temper.*

    _____

4. Caulking the windows, *to replace weather stripping,* and painting the garage are my chores for the weekend. _____

5. With her pale skin and *her eyes that were green,* she appeared ghostly in the moonlight. _____

6. As an Oprah Winfrey fan, I love to watch her show and *reading her magazine.*

    _____

7. After calling the police, checking the area hospitals, and *we prayed,* we could only wait. _____

8. The stars appeared on talk shows, signed autographs, and *were attending* opening nights in order to promote their latest movie. _____

9. Our teenage daughter ties up the phone for hours, giggling with her girlfriends, deciding what to wear, and *complaints about her strict parents.*

    _____

10. In Allan's nightmare, he was audited by the IRS, investigated by the police, and *bill collectors were chasing him.* _____

    _____

Complete the following statements. The first two parts of each statement are parallel in form; the part that you add should be parallel in form as well.

EXAMPLE

Three things I like about myself are my sense of humor, my thoughtfulness, and *my self-discipline.*

1. Among the drawbacks of apartment living are noisy neighbors, yearly rent increases, and _____

2. Three bad habits I have resolved to change are losing my temper, showing up late for appointments, and _____

3. The best features of my part-time job are good pay, flexible hours, and

   _____

4. Cigarette smoking is expensive, disgusting, and _____

5. Lessons I had to learn after moving from my parents' home included how to budget my money, how to take care of my own laundry, and _____

   _____

Collaborative Activity

Editing and Rewriting

Working with a partner, read carefully the short paragraph below and mark the five instances of faulty parallelism. Then use the space provided to correct the instances of faulty parallelism. Feel free to discuss the rewrite quietly with your partner and refer back to the chapter when necessary.

[1]Human beings attempt to protect themselves psychologically as well as in physical ways. [2]If someone harms you physically, you may want to fight back. [3]To guard yourself psychologically, you may use defense mechanisms. [4]You may be unaware of your real motives in adjusting to a situation that is undesirable or a threat. [5]Three common defense mechanisms are regression, rationalization, and trying to compensate.

continued

6Regression means returning to an earlier form of behavior. 7A person who regresses temporarily rejects the "hard cruel world" and is seeking the greater security of childhood. 8Rationalization is making excuses. 9A student not wanting to study for a test decides that she doesn't know what to study. 10Compensation is a form of substitution. 11If a person wants a better education but cannot attend school, she may try studying on her own or to learn more through experience.

_____

_____

_____

_____

_____

_____

_____

_____

_____

_____

_____

_____

_____

_____

_____

Collaborative Activity

Creating Sentences

Working with a partner, make up your own short test on faulty parallelism, as directed.

1. Write a sentence that includes three things you want to do tomorrow. One of those things should not be in parallel form. Then correct the faulty parallelism.

   Nonparallel _____

   _____

   Parellel _____

   _____

2. Write a sentence that names three positive qualities of a person you like or three negative qualities of a person you don't like.

   Nonparallel _____

   _____

   Parellel _____

   _____

3. Write a sentence that includes three everyday things that annoy you.

   Nonparallel _____

   _____

   Parellel _____

   _____

Reflective Activity

1. Look at the paragraph on defense mechanisms that you revised above. How has the attention to parallel form improved the paragraph?

2. How would you evaluate your use of parallel form in your writing? Do you use it almost never, at times, or often? How would you benefit from using it more?

Review Test 1

Cross out the unbalanced part of each sentence. Then rewrite the unbalanced part so that it matches the other item or items in the sentence.

EXAMPLE

I enjoy watering the grass and ~~to work~~ in the garden.

working

1. Our production supervisor warned Jed to punch in on time, dress appropriately for the job, and he should stop taking extra breaks.

_____

2. On his ninetieth birthday, the old man mused that his long life was due to hard work, a loving wife, and because he had a sense of humor.

_____

3. The philosopher's advice is to live for the present, find some joy in each day, and by helping others.

_____

4. Freshly prepared food, an attractive decor, and having prompt service are signs of a good restaurant.

_____

5. Tarah has tickets for reckless driving, speeding, and she parked illegally.

_____

6. Washing clothes, cooking meals, and to take care of children used to be called "women's work."

_____

7. Our compact car provides better mileage; more comfort is provided by our station wagon.

_____

8. As the first bartender to arrive each day, Elena must slice lemons, get ice, and she has to check the inventory.

_____

Guidelines for Preparing a Paper

Here are guidelines to follow in preparing a paper for an instructor.

1. Use full-sized theme or printer paper, 8½ by 11 inches.

2. Leave wide margins (1 to 1½ inches) all around the paper. In particular, do not crowd the right-hand or bottom margin. This white space makes your paper more readable; it also gives the instructor room to write comments.

3. If you write by hand,

   - Use a pen with blue or black ink (*not* a pencil).

   - Be careful not to overlap letters and not to make decorative loops on letters.

   - On narrow-ruled paper, write on every other line.

   - Make all your letters distinct. Pay special attention to *a, e, i, o,* and *u*—five letters that people sometimes write illegibly.

4. Center the title of your paper on the first line of the first page. Do not put quotation marks around the title. Do not underline the title. Capitalize all the major words in a title, including the first word. Short connecting words within a title, such as *of, for, the, in,* and *to,* are not capitalized.

5. Skip a line between the title and the first line of your text. Indent the first line of each paragraph about five spaces (half an inch) from the left-hand margin.

6. Make commas, periods, and other punctuation marks firm and clear. Leave a slight space after each period.

7. If you break a word at the end of a line, break only between syllables (see page 383). Do not break words of one syllable.

8. Put your name, date, and course number where your instructor asks for them.

Remember these points about the title and the first sentence of your paper.

9. The title should be several words that tell what the paper is about. It should usually *not* be a complete sentence. For example, if you are writing a paper about your jealous sister, the title could simply be "My Jealous Sister."

10. Do not rely on the title to help explain the first sentence of your paper. The first sentence must be independent of the title. For instance, if the title of your paper is "My Jealous Sister," the first sentence should *not* be "She has been this way as long as I can remember." Rather, the first sentence might be "My sister has always been a jealous person."

Practice

1

Identify the mistakes in format in the following lines from a student theme. Explain the mistakes in the spaces provided. One mistake is described for you as an example.

	"The generation gap in our house"
	When I was a girl, I never argued with my parents about
	differences between their attitude and mine. My father
	would deliver his judgment on an issue and that was alw-
	ays the end of the matter. There was no discussion permit-
	ted, so I gradually began to express my disagreement in other

1. *Hyphenate only between syllables (al-ways).*

2. _____

3. _____

4. _____

5. _____

6. _____

Practice

2

As already stated, a title should tell in several words what a paper is about. Often a title can be based on the sentence that expresses the main idea of a paper.

Following are five main-idea sentences from student papers. Write a suitable and specific title for each paper, basing the title on the main idea.

EXAMPLE

Title: *Aging Americans as Outcasts*

Our society treats aging Americans as outcasts in many ways.

1. Title: _____
    Selfishness is a common trait in young children.

2. Title: _____
    Exercising every morning offers a number of benefits.

3. Title: _____
    My teenage son is a stubborn person.

4. Title: _____
    To survive in college, a person must learn certain essential study skills.

5. Title: _____
    Only after I married did I fully realize the drawbacks and values of single life.

Names of Persons and the Word *I*

At the picnic, I met Tony Curry and Lola Morrison.

Names of Particular Places

After graduating from Gibbs High School in Houston, I worked for a summer at a nearby Holiday Inn on Clairmont Boulevard.

But Use small letters if the specific name of a place is not given.

After graduating from high school in my hometown, I worked for a summer at a nearby hotel on one of the main shopping streets.

Names of Days of the Week, Months, and Holidays

This year, Memorial Day falls on the last Thursday in May.

But Use small letters for the seasons—summer, fall, winter, spring.

In the early summer and fall, my hay fever bothers me.

Names of Commercial Products

The consumer magazine gave high ratings to Cheerios breakfast cereal, Breyer's ice cream, and Progresso chicken noodle soup.

But Use small letters for the *type* of product (breakfast cereal, ice cream, chicken noodle soup, and the like).

Titles of Books, Magazines, Articles, Films, Television Shows, Songs, Poems, Stories, Papers That You Write, and the Like

My oral report was on *The Diary of a Young Girl*, by Anne Frank.

While watching *The Young and the Restless* on television, I thumbed through *Cosmopolitan* magazine and the *New York Times*.

Names of Companies, Associations, Unions, Clubs, Religious and Political Groups, and Other Organizations

A new bill before Congress is opposed by the National Rifle Association.

My wife is Jewish; I am Roman Catholic. We are both members of the Democratic Party.

My parents have life insurance with Prudential, auto insurance with Allstate, and medical insurance with Blue Cross and Blue Shield.

Write a paragraph describing the advertisement shown here so that a person who has never seen it will be able to visualize it and fully understand it. Once you have written your paragraph, check to make sure you have used capital letters properly throughout.

Practice

1

In the sentences that follow, cross out the words that need capitals. Then write the capitalized forms of the words in the space provided. The number of spaces tells you how many corrections to make in each case.

EXAMPLE

Rhoda said, "why should I bother to *eat* this hershey bar? I should just apply it directly to my hips." _____Why_____ _____Hershey_____

1. Vince wanted to go to the halloween party dressed as a thanksgiving turkey, but he was afraid someone might try to carve him.

   Halloween   Thanksgiving

2. Laurie called upstairs, "if you're not ready in five minutes, i'm leaving without you."

   If   I'm

3. The old ford rattled its way from connecticut to florida on four balding goodyear tires.

   Ford   Connecticut   Florida   goodyear

4. Patients read *newsweek, time,* and *people* magazines while they waited for the dentist to examine them.

   Newsweek   Time   People

5. Juanita King, a member of the northside improvement association, urged the city to clean up the third Street neighborhood.

   Northside   Improvement   Association   Third

6. At soundworks, a discount store on washington boulevard, she purchased a panasonic stereo amplifier.

   Soundworks   Washington   Boulevard   Panasonic

7. Tom finished basic training at fort gordon and was transferred to a base near Stuttgart, germany.

   Fort   Gordon   Germany

8. On thursday nights Terri goes to the weight watchers meeting at a nearby high school.

   Thursday   Weight   Watchers

9. The two films they enjoyed most during the horror film festival held in february were *return* of *dracula* and *alien*.

   February   Return   Dracula   Alien

10. My sister bought jeans at old navy and got lunch at taco bell.

    Old   Navy   Taco   Bell

Other Uses of Capital Letters

Capital letters are also used with

1. Names that show family relationships
2. Titles of persons when used with their names
3. Specific school courses
4. Languages
5. Geographic locations
6. Historical periods and events
7. Races, nations, and nationalities
8. The opening and closing of a letter

Each use is illustrated on the pages that follow.

Names That Show Family Relationships

Aunt Fern and Uncle Jack are selling their house.

I asked Grandfather to start the fire.

Is Mom feeling better?

But Do not capitalize words like *mother, father, grandmother, grandfather, uncle, aunt,* and so on when they are preceded by *my* or another possessive word.

My aunt and uncle are selling their house.

I asked my grandfather to start the fire.

Is my mom feeling better?

Titles of Persons When Used with Their Names

I wrote a letter to President Barack Obama questioning his decisions about health care.

Can you drive to Dr. Parehk's office?

We asked Professor Bushkin about his attendance policy.

But Use small letters when titles appear by themselves, without specific names.

I wrote an angry letter to my senator.

Can you drive to the doctor's office?

We asked our professor about his attendance policy.

Specific School Courses

My courses this semester include Accounting I, Introduction to Web Design, Business Law, General Psychology, and Basic Math.

But Use small letters for general subject areas.

This semester I'm taking mostly business courses, but I have a psychology course and a math course as well.

Languages

Yasmin speaks English and Spanish equally well.

Geographic Locations

I lived in the South for many years and then moved to the West Coast.

But Use small letters in giving directions.

Go south for about five miles and then bear west.

Historical Periods and Events

One essay question dealt with the Civil Rights Movement in the United States.

Races, Nations, Nationalities

The census form asked whether I was Caucasian, African American, Native American, Latino, or Asian.

Last summer I hitchhiked through Italy, France, and Germany.

The city is a melting pot for Koreans, Vietnamese, and Mexican Americans.

But Use small letters when referring to *whites* or *blacks.*

Both whites and blacks supported our mayor in the election.

Opening and Closing of a Letter

Dear Sir:	Sincerely yours,
Dear Madam:	Truly yours,

TIP Capitalize only the first word in a closing.

Practice

2

Cross out the words that need capitals in the following sentences. Then write the capitalized forms of the words in the spaces provided. The number of spaces tells you how many corrections to make in each case.

1. When ~~aunt esther~~ died, she left all her money to her seven cats and nothing to my uncle.

    Aunt   _Esther_

2. This fall I'm taking night courses in ~~spanish~~ and ~~aerobic exercise~~ I.

    Spanish _Aerobic_ _Exercise_

3. Tony was referred to ~~dr. purdy~~'s office because his regular dentist was on vacation.

    _Dr._   _Purdy_

4. The ~~latino~~ family in the apartment upstairs has just moved here from the ~~southwest~~.

    Latino   _Southwest_

5. My accounting courses are giving me less trouble than ~~intermediate math~~ 201.

    Intermediate _Math_

Unnecessary Use of Capitals

Practice

3

Many errors in capitalization are caused by adding capitals where they are not needed. Cross out the incorrectly capitalized letters in the following sentences and write the correct forms in the spaces provided. The number of spaces tells you how many corrections to make in each sentence.

1. During the ~~Summer~~ I like to sit in my backyard, ~~Sunbathe~~, and read ~~Magazines~~ like *Glamour* and *People*.

    summer   _sunbathe_ _magazines_

2. Every ~~Week~~ I seem to be humming another ~~Tune~~. Lately I have been humming the ~~Melody~~ for the latest Pepsi commercial on television.

    week   _tune_   _melody_

3. After ~~High School~~ I traveled to twenty ~~States~~, including Alaska, and then I decided to enroll in a local ~~College~~.

    States   _high_   _school_   _college_

4. *The tires belonging to the cars* are badly worn.

_____

5. *The bicycle owned by Joe* was stolen from the bike rack outside school.

   Joe's bicycle

6. I discovered the *nest of the blue jay* while pruning the tree.

_____

7. I don't like *the title of my paper.*

   paper's title

8. *The arthritis of my mother* gets progressively worse.

   mother's arthritis

9. *The boyfriend belonging to my sister* is a gorgeous-looking man.

   My sister's boyfriend

10. It is *a game belonging to anybody* at this point.

   anybody's game

Underline the word in each sentence that needs an *'s*. Then write the word correctly in the space at the left. One is done for you as an example.

Practice 6

children's   1. The children voices carried downstairs.

Georgia's   2. Georgia husband is not a take-charge guy.

friend's   3. My friend computer is also a typewriter.

teacher's   4. When the teacher anger became apparent, the class quickly grew quiet.

girlfriend's   5. His girlfriend apple pie made his stomach rebel.

Albert's   6. Albert dog looks like a porcupine without its quills.

daughter's   7. Under the couch were several of our daughter toys.

boss's   8. My boss car was stolen.

night's   9. That wine tastes like last night rain.

son's   10. The dentist charged $75 to fix our son tooth.

Add an *'s* to each of the following words to make it the possessor or owner of something. Then write sentences using the words. Your sentences can be serious or playful. One is done for you as an example.

1. Cary _____ *Cary's* _____

   _____ *Cary's hair is bright red.* _____

2. neighbor __ neighbor's __

   _____

3. car _____ car's _____

   _____

4. sister _____ sister's _____

   _____

5. doctor _____ doctor's _____

   _____

Apostrophe versus Possessive Pronouns

Do not use an apostrophe with possessive pronouns. They already show ownership. Possessive pronouns include *his, hers, its, yours, ours,* and *theirs.*

Incorrect	Correct
The bookstore lost its' lease.	The bookstore lost its lease.
The racing bikes were theirs'.	The racing bikes were theirs.
The change is yours'.	The change is yours.
His' problems are ours', too.	His problems are ours, too.
Her' cold is worse than his'.	Her cold is worse than his.

Apostrophe versus Simple Plurals

When you want to make a word plural, just add an *s* at the end of the word. Do *not* add an apostrophe. For example, the plural of the word *movie* is *movies,* not *movie's* or *movies'.* Look at this sentence:

When Korie's cat began catching birds, the neighbors called the police.

The words *birds* and *neighbors* are simple plurals, meaning more than one bird, more than one neighbor. The plural is shown by adding *-s* only. (More information about plurals starts on page 396.) On the other hand, the *'s* after *Korie* shows possession—that Korie owns the cat.

Why is this cartoon funny?

In the spaces provided under each sentence, add the one apostrophe needed and explain why the other words ending in *s* are simple plurals.

Practice

8

EXAMPLE

Originally, the cuffs of mens pants were meant for cigar ashes.

cuffs: *simple plural meaning more than one cuff*

mens: *men's, meaning "belonging to men"*

ashes: *simple plural meaning more than one ash*

1. The sharp odor of the cheese and onions made Rons eyes water.

   onions: more than one onion (plural)

   Rons: belonging

   eyes: _____

2. My mothers recipe for chicken pot pie is famous among our relatives and friends.

   mothers: belonging

   relatives: more than one plural

   friends: plural

3. Sailors ran to their battle stations; the ships alarm had sounded.

   Sailors: _belonging / plural_

   stations: _plural_

   ships: _possessive_

4. The kites string broke when it got caught in the branches of a tree.

   kites: _possessive_

   branches: _plural_

5. We met two guys after our colleges football game and went with them to the movies that night.

   guys: _plural_

   colleges: _possessive_

   movies: _plural_

6. My daughters prayers were answered when the heavy snow caused all the schools in the area to close for the rest of the week.

   daughters: _possessive_

   prayers: _plural_

   schools: _plural_

7. We almost drowned when our inner tubes turned over in the rivers rushing currents.

   tubes: _plural_

   rivers: _possessive_

   currents: _plural_

8. That movie directors specialty is films about vampires.

   directors: _possessive_

   films: _plural_

   vampires: _plural_

9. The secretary made copies of the companys tax returns for the previous three years.

copies: _____plural_____

companys: _____possessive_____

returns: _____

years: _____plural_____

10. Scientists are exploring Africas Congo region for living relatives of the dinosaurs.

Scientists: _____plural_____

Africas: _____possessive_____

relatives: _____plural_____

dinosaurs: _____plural_____

Apostrophe with Plural Words Ending in -s

Plurals that end in *-s* show possession simply by adding the apostrophe, rather than an apostrophe plus *s*.

Both of my *neighbors'* homes have been burglarized recently.

The many *workers'* complaints were ignored by the company.

All the *campers'* tents were damaged by the hailstorm.

www.mhhe.com/langan

In each sentence, cross out the one plural word that needs an apostrophe. Then write the word correctly, with the apostrophe, in the space provided.

Practice

9

EXAMPLE

_____bosses'_____ My two ~~bosses~~ tempers are much the same: explosive.

firefighters' 1. Icy water from the hose froze on many of the firefighters coats.

drivers' 2. Other drivers mistakes have led to my three car accidents.

friends' 3. Two of my friends cars have been stolen recently.

grandparents' 4. My grandparents television has a fifty-inch screen.

soldiers' 5. All of the soldiers uniforms will be replaced.

Collaborative Activity

Editing and Rewriting

Working with a partner, read the short paragraph below. Then use the space provided to rewrite the paragraph, adding ten apostrophes where needed to indicate contractions and possessives. Feel free to discuss the rewrite quietly with your partner and refer back to the chapter when necessary.

¹In a small park near the center of Millville, several bronze statues stand in a circle. ²Most of them are models of the individual rich men who provided money for the towns beginning. ³The center of the circle is occupied by a nameless man. ⁴Citizens call him Joe because hes a symbol of the common man. ⁵Joes clothes appear tattered, but his body seems strong. ⁶His face looks tired, but his eyes look proud. ⁷Each person Joe represents couldnt give money to the town but gave strength and sweat instead. ⁸A farmers back worked to supply food to the town. ⁹A womans hands wove, knitted, and sewed clothes. ¹⁰A blacksmiths arms struggled to provide horseshoes and tools. ¹¹Joes eyes must talk to passersby. ¹²People seem to realize that without the ordinary persons help, the circle of rich men wouldnt exist.

_____

_____

_____

_____

_____

_____

_____

_____

_____

_____

NAME: _____

DATE: _____

Apostrophe MASTERY TEST 2

In the space provided under each sentence, add the one apostrophe needed and explain why the other word ending in *s* is a simple plural.

EXAMPLE

Joans hair began to fall out two days after she dyed it.

Joans: _Joan's meaning "hair belonging to Joan"_____

days: _simple plural meaning more than one day_____

1. The students gradually got used to the professors Japanese accent.

    students: _____

    professors: _____

2. Our tough sheriffs campaign promise is that he'll replace the electric chair with electric bleachers.

    sheriffs: _____

    bleachers: _____

3. My little sisters habit of sucking in noodles makes her an unpleasant dining companion.

    sisters: _____

    noodles: _____

4. When the students complained about the instructors assignment, he said, "You're not in high school anymore."

    students: _____

    instructors: _____

5. A football-sized nest of yellow jackets hung menacingly under the roofs rain gutter.

    jackets: _____

    roofs: _____

NAME: _____

DATE: _____

MASTERY TEST 3 ## Apostrophe

In each sentence two apostrophes are missing or are used incorrectly. Cross out the two errors and write the corrections in the spaces provided.

_____
_____
1. Terrences day started going sour when he noticed that everyone in the donut shop had gotten fatter donuts' than he got.

_____
_____
2. While the team was in the showers, someone tied all the players sneakers' together.

you'll
I'll
3. If youll check the noise in the attic, Ill stand by the phone in case you scream.

_____
_____
4. Despite the drivers warning that smoking was not allowed, several people lit cigarettes' in the back of the bus.

_____
_____
5. When I sat on the fender of Hassans car, he stared darts' at me until I slid off.

_____
_____
6. My brothers cell phone was stolen by vandals' who broke his car window.

_____
_____
7. Melissas typing might improve if shed cut an inch off her nails.

_____
_____
8. Anna has been on Andys blacklist since she revealed that he sleeps with his' socks on.

_____
_____
9. The troopers face was stern as he told me that my drivers license had expired.

_____
_____
10. I never ride anymore in my uncles station wagon; its like being on a roller coaster.

NAME: _____

DATE: _____

Apostrophe MASTERY TEST 4

In each sentence two apostrophes are missing or are used incorrectly. Cross out
the two errors and write the corrections in the spaces provided.

_____ 1. I was shocked when the movie stars toupee blew off; I hadnt realized he was
completely bald.

_____ 2. The skirts cheap lining puckered and scorched even though Eileens iron was
set at the lowest possible heat level.

_____ 3. The two boys boat capsized in the rivers rushing current.

_____ 4. Teds work always ends up on someone elses desk.

_____ 5. People in the dentists waiting room squirmed uneasily as a childs cries
echoed down the hall.

_____ 6. When Jeans voice cracked during her solo, I thought shed faint with
embarrassment.

_____ 7. Didnt you know that school will be closed next week because of a teachers
conference?

_____ 8. My youngest sisters goldfish has jumped out of its' bowl many times.

_____ 9. "Its the muffler," the mechanic explained, crawling out from under Freds
car.

_____ 10. Kevin knew he was headed for trouble when his dates father said that hed
like to come along.

Quotation Marks

25

Read the following scene and underline all the words enclosed within quotation marks. Your instructor may also have you dramatize the scene with one person reading the narration and three persons acting the speaking parts—Len, Tina, and Mario. The two speakers should imagine the scene as part of a stage play and try to make their words seem as real and true-to-life as possible.

At a party that Len and his wife Tina recently hosted, Len got angry at a guy named Mario who kept bothering Tina. "Listen, man," Len said, "what's this thing you have for my wife? There are lots of other women at this party."

"Relax," Mario replied. "Tina is very attractive, and I enjoy talking with her."

"Listen, Mario," Tina said. "I've already told you three times that I don't want to talk to you anymore. Please leave me alone."

"Look, there's no law that says I can't talk to you if I want to," Mario challenged.

"Mario, I'm only going to say this once," Len warned. "Lay off my wife, or leave this party *now*."

Mario grinned at Len smugly. "You've got good liquor here. Why should I leave? Besides, I'm not done talking with Tina."

Len went to his basement and was back a minute later holding a two-by-four. "I'm giving you a choice," Len said. "Leave by the door or I'll slam you out the window."

Mario left by the door.

1. On the basis of the above selection, what is the purpose of quotation marks?

   _____

2. Do commas and periods that come after a quotation go inside or outside the quotation marks?

   _____

Answers are on page 571.

The two main uses of quotation marks are:

1. To set off the exact words of a speaker or writer

2. To set off the titles of short works

Each use is explained on the pages that follow.

Quotation Marks to Set Off the Words of a Speaker or Writer

www.mhhe.com/langan

Use quotation marks when you want to show the exact words of a speaker or writer:

"Who left the cap off the toothpaste?" Lola demanded. (Quotation marks set off the exact words that Lola spoke.)

Ben Franklin wrote, "Keep your eyes wide open before marriage, half shut afterward." (Quotation marks set off the exact words that Ben Franklin wrote.)

"You're never too young," my Aunt Fern often tells me, "to have a heart attack." (Two pairs of quotation marks are used to enclose the aunt's exact words.)

Maria complained, "I look so old some days. Even makeup doesn't help. I feel as though I'm painting a corpse!" (Note that the end quotes do not come until the end of Maria's speech. Place quotation marks before the first quoted word of a speech and after the last quoted word. As long as no interruption occurs in the speech, do not use quotation marks for each new sentence.)

Complete the following statements that explain how capital letters, commas, and periods are used in quotations. Refer to the four examples on the previous page as guides.

> **HINT** In the four preceding examples, notice that a comma sets off the quoted part from the rest of the sentence. Also observe that commas and periods at the end of a quotation always go *inside* quotation marks.

- Every quotation begins with a _____ letter.

- When a quotation is split (as in the sentence about Aunt Fern), the second part does not begin with a capital letter unless it is a _____ sentence.

- _____ are used to separate the quoted part of a sentence from the rest of the sentence.

- Commas and periods that come at the end of a quote go _____ quotation marks.

The answers are *capital, new, Commas,* and *inside.*

Practice 1

Insert quotation marks where needed in the sentences that follow.

1. Have more trust in me, Lola said to her mother.
2. The instructor asked Sharon, Why are your eyes closed?
3. Christ said, I come that you may have life, and have it more abundantly.
4. I refuse to wear those itchy wool pants! Ralph shouted at his parents.
5. His father replied, We should give all the clothes you never wear to the Salvation Army.
6. The nervous boy whispered hoarsely over the telephone, Is Linda home?
7. When I was ten, Lola said, I spent my entire summer playing Monopoly.
8. Tony said, When I was ten, I spent my whole summer playing basketball.
9. The critic wrote about the play, It runs the gamut of emotions from A to B.
10. The best way to tell if a mushroom is poisonous, the doctor solemnly explained, is if you find it in the stomach of a dead person.

Rewrite the following sentences, adding quotation marks where needed. Use a capital letter to begin a quotation, and use a comma to set off a quoted part from the rest of the sentence.

Practice 2

EXAMPLE

I'm getting tired Sally said.

"I'm getting tired," Sally said.

1. Greg said I'm going with you.

   Greg said," I'm going with you".

2. Everyone passed the test the instructor informed the class.

3. My parents asked where were you?

4. I hate that commercial he muttered.

5. If you don't leave soon, he warned, you'll be late for work.

Practice 3

1. Write three quotations that appear in the first part of a sentence.

EXAMPLE

"Let's go shopping," I suggested.

   a.

   b.

   c.

2. Write three quotations that appear at the end of a sentence.

EXAMPLE

Bob asked, "Have you had lunch yet?"

   a.

   b.

   c.

3. Write three quotations that appear at the beginning and end of a sentence.

EXAMPLE

"If the bus doesn't come soon," Mary said, "we'll freeze."

a. _____

b. _____

c. _____

Indirect Quotations

An indirect quotation is a rewording of someone else's comments rather than a word-for-word direct quotation. The word *that* often signals an indirect quotation.

Direct Quotation	Indirect Quotation
George said, "My son is a dare-devil."	George said that his son is a dare-devil.
(George's exact spoken words are given, so quotation marks are used.)	(We learn George's words *in*directly, so no quotation marks are used.)
Carol's note to Arnie read, "I'm at the neighbors' house. Give me a call."	Carol left a note for Arnie that said that she would be at the neighbors' house and he should give her a call.
(The exact words that Carol wrote in the note are given, so quotation marks are used.)	(We learn Carol's words *in*directly, so no quotation marks are used.)

Practice

4

Rewrite the following sentences, changing words as necessary to convert the sentences into direct quotations. The first one is done for you as an example.

1. Eric asked Lynn if she had mailed the party invitations.

    Eric asked Lynn, "Have you mailed the party invitations?"

2. Lynn replied that she thought Eric was going to write them this year.

    _____

3. Eric said that writing invitations was a woman's job.

    _____

4. Lynn exclaimed that Eric was crazy.

   _____

5. Eric replied that she had much better handwriting than he did.

   _____

Rewrite the following sentences, converting each direct quotation into an indirect statement. In each case you will have to add the word *that* or *if* and change other words as well.

EXAMPLE

   The barber asked Reggie, "Have you noticed how your hair is thinning?"

   The barber asked Reggie if he had noticed how his hair was thinning.

1. He said, "As the plane went higher, my heart sank lower."

   _____

2. The designer said, "Shag rugs are back in style."

   _____

3. The foreman asked Susan, "Have you ever operated a lift truck?"

   _____

4. My new neighbor asked, "Would you like to come over for coffee?"

   _____

5. Mei Lin complained, "I married a man who eats Tweeties cereal for breakfast."

   _____

   _____

Quotation Marks to Set Off the Titles of Short Works

www.mhhe.com/langan

Titles of short works are usually set off by quotation marks, while titles of long works are underlined. Use quotation marks to set off the titles of such short works as articles in books, newspapers, or magazines; chapters in a book; short stories; poems; and songs. On the other hand, you should underline the titles of books, newspapers, magazines, plays, movies, compact discs, and television shows. See the following examples.

Quotation Marks

the article "The Toxic Tragedy"

the article "New Cures for Head-aches"

the article "When the Patient Plays Doctor"

the chapter "Connecting with Kids"

the story "The Dead"

the poem "Birches"

the song "Some Enchanted Evening"

Underlines

in the book <u>Who's Poisoning America</u>

in the newspaper <u>The New York Times</u>

in the magazine <u>Family Health</u>

in the book <u>Straight Talk</u>

in the book <u>Dubliners</u>

in the book <u>The Complete Poems of Robert Frost</u>

in the album <u>South Pacific</u>

the television show <u>Jeopardy</u>

the movie <u>Rear Window</u>

TIP In printed form, the titles of long works are set off by italics—slanted type that looks *like this.*

Practice 6

Use quotation marks or underlines as needed.

1. The young couple opened their brand-new copy of Cooking Made Easy to the chapter titled Meat Loaf Magic.

2. Annabelle borrowed Hawthorne's novel The Scarlet Letter from the library because she thought it was about a varsity athlete.

3. Did you know that the musical West Side Story is actually a modern version of Shakespeare's tragedy Romeo and Juliet?

4. I used to think that Richard Connell's short story The Most Dangerous Game was the scariest piece of suspense fiction in existence—until I began reading Bram Stoker's classic novel Dracula.

5. Every year at Easter, we watch a movie such as The Robe on television.

6. During the past year, Time featured an article about DNA titled Building Blocks of the Future.

7. My father still remembers the way Sarah Brightman sang "Think of Me" in the original production of The Phantom of the Opera.

8. As I stand in the supermarket checkout line, I read a feature story in the National Enquirer titled Mother Gives Birth to Alien Baby.

9. My favorite song by Aretha Franklin is the classic Respect, which has been included in the CD Aretha's Best.

10. Absentmindedly munching a Dorito, Hana opened the latest issue of Newsweek to its cover story, The Junk Food Explosion.

Other Uses of Quotation Marks

1. **To set off special words or phrases from the rest of a sentence:**

   Many people spell the words "all right" as one word, "alright," instead of correctly spelling them as two words.

   I have trouble telling the difference between "principal" and "principle."

www.mhhe.com/langan

2. **To mark off a quote within a quote. For this purpose, single quotes (' ') are used:**

   Ben Franklin said, "The noblest question in the world is, 'What good may I do in it?' "

   "If you want to have a scary experience," Eric told Lynn, "read Stephen King's story 'The Mangler' in his book Night Shift."

Collaborative Activity

Editing and Rewriting

Working with a partner, read the short passage below and circle the ten sets of quotation mark mistakes. Then use the space provided to rewrite the passage, adding the ten sets of quotation marks. Feel free to discuss the rewrite quietly with your partner and refer back to the chapter when necessary.

¹Holding a container of milk and a bag of potatoes, Tony and Lola were standing in the express line at the Safeway supermarket. ²Lola pointed to a sign above the checkout counter that read, Express line—ten items or less. ³She then said to Tony, Look at that guy ahead of us. ⁴He shouldn't be in the express lane.

⁵Be quiet, said Tony. ⁶If you're not, he'll hear you.

⁷I don't mind if he does hear me, Lola replied. ⁸People like that think the world owes them a favor. ⁹I hope the cashier makes him go to another lane. ¹⁰The man in front of them suddenly turned around. ¹¹Stop acting as if I've committed a federal crime, he said. ¹²See those five cans of Alpo—that counts as one item. ¹³See those four packs of Twinkies—that's one item. ¹⁴Let's just say this, Lola replied. ¹⁵You have an interesting way of counting.

_____

_____

_____

_____

_____

_____

_____

_____

_____

_____

Creating Sentences

Working with a partner, write sentences that use quotation marks as directed.

1. Write a sentence in which you quote a favorite expression of someone you know. Identify the person's relationship to you.

    EXAMPLE

    My brother Sam often says after a meal, "That wasn't bad at all."

    _____

    _____

    _____

2. Write a quotation that contains the words *Tony asked Lola*. Write a second quotation that includes the words *Lola replied*.

    _____

    _____

    _____

3. Write a sentence that interests or amuses you from a book, magazine, or newspaper. Identify the title and author of the book, magazine, or newspaper article.

    EXAMPLE

    In her book <u>At Wit's End</u>, Erma Bombeck advises, "Never go to a doctor whose office plants have died."

    _____

    _____

    _____

Reflective Activity

1. Look at the passage about the checkout line that you revised above. Explain how adding quotation marks has affected the reading of the passage.

2. What would writing be like without quotation marks? Explain, using an example, how quotation marks are important to understanding writing.

3. Explain what it is about quotation marks that is most difficult for you to remember and apply. Use an example to make your point clear. Feel free to refer back to anything in this chapter.

Review Test   1

Place quotation marks around the exact words of a speaker or writer in the sentences that follow.

1. Are you seeing what I'm seeing? the friends asked each other.

2. Murphy's law states, Whatever can go wrong, will.

3. John Kennedy once said, Ask not what your country can do for you; ask what you can do for your country.

4. The sign read, Be careful how you drive. You may meet a fool.

5. Martha said, Turn on the burglar alarm when you leave the house, Fred.

6. Tony asked the struggling old lady if he could help with her heavy bag. Go to blazes, you masher, she said.

7. Listen, I confided to my sister, Neil told me he is going to ask you to go out with him.

8. The sign in the tough Western saloon read, Carry out your own dead.

9. When the ball hit Willie Wilson in the head and bounced into the outfield, Eric remarked, That was a heads-up play.

10. A woman who was one of Winston Churchill's political enemies once remarked to him, If you were my husband, I would put poison in your coffee. Churchill's reply was, Madam, if I were your husband, I would drink it.

Review Test 2

Go through the comics section of a newspaper to find a comic strip that amuses you. Be sure to choose a strip where two or more characters are speaking to each other. Write a full description that will enable people who have not read the comic strip to visualize it clearly and appreciate its humor. Describe the setting and action in each panel and enclose the words of the speakers in quotation marks.

NAME: _____

DATE: _____

MASTERY TEST 1 | Quotation Marks

Place quotation marks where needed.

1. A friend of mine used to say, There's nothing wrong with you that a few birthdays won't cure.

2. The food critic wrote, The best test of a fast-food hamburger is to eat it after all the trimmings have been taken off.

3. After I finished James Thurber's story The Secret Life of Walter Mitty, I started to write a paper on it.

4. Poet and writer Maya Angelou said, When people show you who they are, believe them.

5. Well, this is just fine, he mumbled. The recipe calls for four eggs and I have only two.

6. Eating Lola's chili, Tony whispered, is a breathtaking experience.

7. After Bill pulled the flip-top cap off the can, he noticed that the label said, Shake well before drinking.

8. How would you feel, the instructor asked the class, if I gave you a surprise quiz today?

9. In a tired voice, Clyde asked, Did you ever wonder why kids have more energy at the end of a long day than they had when they got up?

10. When Dick Cavett first met Groucho Marx on a street corner, he said, Hello, Groucho, I'm a big fan of yours. Groucho's response was, If it gets any hotter, I could use a big fan.

NAME: _____

DATE: _____

Quotation Marks MASTERY TEST 2

Place quotation marks or underlines where needed.

1. The tag on the pillow read, Do not remove under penalty of law.

2. Experts say the H1N1 vaccine is safe, said Ella. However, I'm still not getting the shot.

3. If we don't hurry, we'll miss the beginning of the movie, Joe reminded Liz.

4. Honest men, said the cranky old man, are scarcer than the feathers on a frog.

5. The most famous line from George Orwell's novel 1984 is Big Brother is watching you.

6. It never fails, complained Martha. Just as I lie down to take a nap, the telephone rings.

7. I know I'm getting old, Grandfather said. When I walked past the cemetery today, two guys ran after me with shovels.

8. There is a sign in the grocery store that reads, In God we trust. All others pay cash.

9. When Clyde got home from work, he said, At times I feel I'm in a rat race and the rats are winning. Charlotte consoled him by saying that everyone feels that way from time to time.

10. In a Consumer Reports article titled What's Inside Frozen Pot Pies? the editors write, The filth we discovered is not a health hazard. But it's unpleasant to discover that these pies contain big and little parts of aphids, flies, moths, weevils, cereal beetles, and rodent hairs.

MASTERY TEST 3 | Quotation Marks

Place quotation marks or underlines where needed.

1. Martin Luther King, Jr., once said, Hate cannot drive out hate; only love can do that.

2. Diana Ross's song It's My Turn is one of my all-time favorites.

3. Are you positive you locked the front door? asked Vince for the third time.

4. You know, William said to the bartender, there are times in my life when I kind of panic. I want to go to bed and never get up again.

5. When I know I have a long day ahead, Judy said, I always have trouble sleeping well the night before.

6. Cracking his knuckles, Herschel complained, I wish people didn't have so many annoying habits.

7. Look out, you idiot! screamed the frightened pedestrian. Are you trying to kill somebody?

8. Immanuel Kant once wrote: Two things fill me with constantly increasing admiration and awe the longer and more earnestly I reflect on them—the starry heavens without and the moral law within.

9. The saying we learned in school was, Do unto others as you would have them do unto you. The saying that I now have on the wall of my study reads, Remember the golden rule: he who has the gold makes the rules.

10. One of the questions in Sharon's American literature test was to identify the book in which the following line appears: You don't know about me without you have read a book by the name of The Adventures of Tom Sawyer, but that ain't no matter.

NAME: _____

DATE: _____

Quotation Marks MASTERY TEST 4

Place quotation marks or underlines where needed.

1. Although I grew up in very modest and challenging circumstances, I consider my life immeasurably rich, said Supreme Court Justice Sonia Sotomayor.

2. The preacher began his sermon with the words, Nobody will ever get out of this world alive.

3. I won't get nervous. I won't get nervous, Terry kept repeating to herself as she walked into the exam room.

4. The honest politician proclaimed to the crowd, I haven't the slightest idea of what I'm talking about.

5. Tony said to Lola, Guess how many jelly beans I can hold in my mouth at one time.

6. Ved complained, No one wants to go with me to Maniac for Hire, the new movie at the multiplex.

7. If an infielder makes a mistake during a softball game, Darryl yells from the bench, You're a disgrace to your base!

8. As a child I was ugly, said the comedian. Once my old man took me to the zoo. The guy at the gate thanked him for returning me.

9. Don't let your paintbrushes dry up, advises the book Saving Money around the House. Instead, store them in motor oil.

10. I agree that the public has a right to know what is in a hot dog, said the president of the meat company. But does the public really want to know what's in a hot dog?

Comma

Introductory Activity

Commas often (though not always) signal a minor break or pause in a sentence. Each of the six pairs of sentences below illustrates one of six main uses of the comma. Read each pair of sentences and choose the rule that applies from the box on the next page. Each of these rules will be discussed in detail in the pages that follow.

_a_ 1. We stocked up on batteries, water, and canned food before the snowstorm.

You can use a credit card, write out a check, or provide cash.

_b_ 2. To open the medicine bottle, press down on the cap and turn it to the right.

Before you lounge in the sun, apply suntan lotion to your body and face.

_c_ 3. Leeches, creatures that suck human blood, are valuable to medical science.

John Nelson, the famous actor, was a classmate of mine.

_d_ 4. Kira said the exam was easy, but I thought it was very difficult.

Wind howled through the alleys, and rain pounded against the roof.

_e_ 5. Terrence asked, "Why is it so hard to remember your dreams the next day?"

"I am so tired after school," Lily said, "that I fall asleep right away."

Add commas to set off interrupting words.

Practice 5

1. Friday is the deadline, the absolute final deadline, for your papers to be turned in.
2. The nursery rhyme told how the cow, a weird creature, jumped over the moon. The rhyme also related how the dish, who must also have been strange, ran away with the spoon.
3. Tod voted the most likely to succeed, in our high school graduating class, has just made the front page of our newspaper. He was arrested with other members of the King Kongs, a local motorcycle gang, for creating a disturbance in the park.

For each item, cross out the one comma that is not needed. Add the two commas that are needed to set off interrupting words.

Practice 6

1. My sister's cat, which she got from the animal shelter, woke her, when her apartment caught fire.
2. A bulging biology textbook, its pages stuffed with notes, and handouts, lay on the path to the college parking lot.
3. A baked potato, with its crispy skin and soft inside, rates as one of my all-time favorite, foods.

Comma between Complete Thoughts Connected by a Joining Word

Use a comma between two complete thoughts connected by *and, but, for, or, nor, so, yet.*

> My parents threatened to throw me out of the house, so I had to stop playing the drums.
>
> The polyester bed sheets had a gorgeous design on them, but they didn't feel as comfortable as plain cotton sheets.
>
> The teenage girls walked the hot summer streets, and the teenage boys drove by in their shined-up cars.

The comma is optional when the complete thoughts are short:

> Calvin relaxed but Robert kept working.
>
> The soda was flat so I poured it away.
>
> We left school early for the furnace broke down.

Be careful not to use a comma in sentences having *one* subject and a *double* verb. The comma is used only in sentences made up of two complete thoughts (two subjects and two verbs). In the sentence

Tamika lay awake that stormy night and listened to the thunder crashing

there is only one subject (*Dawn*) and a double verb (*lay* and *listened*). No comma is needed. Likewise, the sentence

The quarterback kept the ball and plunged across the goal line for a touch-down

has only one subject (*quarterback*) and a double verb (*kept* and *plunged*); therefore, no comma is needed.

Practice

7

Place a comma before a joining word that connects two complete thoughts (two subjects and two verbs). The four sentences that have only one subject and a double verb do not need commas; mark these C for "correct."

1. The outfielder raced to the warning track and caught the fly ball over his shoulder. C

2. The sun set in a golden glow behind the mountain, and a single star sparkled in the night sky.

3. Arturo often tries to cut back on his eating, but he always gives up after a few days.

4. Her voice became very dry during the long speech, and beads of perspiration began to appear on her forehead.

5. Cheryl learned two computer languages in high school, and then began writing her own programs. C

6. I spent all of Saturday morning trying to fix my car, but I still wound up taking it to a garage in the afternoon.

7. She felt like shouting, but didn't dare open her mouth. C

8. He's making a good living selling cosmetics to beauty shops, but he still has regrets about not having gone to college.

9. Crazy Bill often goes into bars, and asks people to buy him a drink. C

10. He decided not to take the course in advanced math, for he wanted to have time for a social life during the semester.

Comma with Direct Quotations

Use a comma to set off a direct quotation from the rest of a sentence.

"Please take a number," said the deli clerk.

Fred told Martha, "I've just signed up for a Dale Carnegie course."

"Those who sling mud," a famous politician once said, "usually lose ground."

"Reading this book," complained Francesca, "is about as interesting as watching paint dry."

TIP A comma or a period at the end of a quotation goes inside quotation marks. See also pages 339–340.

In each sentence, add the one or more commas needed to set off the quoted material.

Practice 8

1. "I can't wait to have a fish filet and some fries," said Lola to Tony as she pulled into the order lane at the fast-food restaurant. She asked, "What can I get you, Tony?"

2. "Two quarter-pounders with cheese, two large fries, and a large Coke," responded Tony.

3. "Good grief," said Lola. "It's hard to believe you don't weigh three hundred pounds. In fact," she continued, "how much do you weigh?"

In each item, cross out the one comma that is not needed to set off a quotation. Add the comma that is needed to set off a quotation from the rest of the sentence.

Practice 9

1. "You better hurry," Thelma's mother warned, "or you're going to miss the last bus of the morning."

2. "It really worries me," said Marty, "that you haven't seen a doctor about that strange swelling under your arm."

3. The student sighed in frustration and then raised his hand. "My computer has crashed again," he called out to the instructor.

Comma with Everyday Material

Use a comma with certain everyday material as shown in the following sections.

Persons Spoken To

Sally, I think that you should go to bed.

Please turn down the stereo, Mark.

Please, sir, can you spare a dollar?

Dates

My best friend got married on April 29, 2005, and he became a parent on January 7, 2007.

Addresses

Lola's sister lives at Greenway Village, 342 Red Oak Drive, Los Angeles, California 90057.

> **TIP** No comma is used before the zip code.

Openings and Closings of Letters

Dear Vanessa,   Sincerely,

Dear John,   Truly yours,

> **TIP** In formal letters, a colon is used after the opening:
>
> Dear Sir:
>
> Dear Madam:

Numbers

Government officials estimate that Americans spend about 785,000,000 hours a year filling out federal forms.

Practice

10

Place commas where needed.

1. I am sorry sir, but you cannot sit at this table.

2. On May 6, 1954, Roger Bannister became the first person to run a mile in under four minutes.

3. Redeeming the savings certificate before June 30, 2010 will result in a substantial penalty.

4. A cash refund of one dollar can be obtained by sending proof of purchase to Seven Seas, P.O. Box 760, El Paso, TX. 79972.

5. Leo get out of bed and come to the lecture with me!

Unnecessary Use of Commas

Remember that if no clear rule applies for using a comma, it is usually better not to use a comma. As stated earlier, "When in doubt, leave it out." Following are some typical examples of unnecessary commas.

Incorrect
Sharon told me, that my socks were different colors. (A comma is not used before *that* unless the flow of thought is interrupted.)

The union negotiations, dragged on for three days. (Do not use a comma between a simple subject and verb.)

I waxed all the furniture, and cleaned the windows. (Use a comma before *and* only with more than two items in a series or when *and* joins two complete thoughts.)

Sharon carried, the baby into the house. (Do not use a comma between a verb and its object.)

I had a clear view, of the entire robbery. (Do not use a comma before a prepositional phrase.)

Cross out the one comma that does not belong in each sentence. Do not add any commas.

1. When I arrived to help with the moving, Jerome said to me, that the work was already done.

2. After the flour and milk have been mixed, eggs must be added, to the recipe.

3. Because my sister is allergic to cat fur, and dust, our family does not own a cat or have any dust-catching drapes or rugs.

4. The guys on the corner, asked, "Have you ever taken karate lessons?"

5. As the heavy Caterpillar tractor, rumbled up the street, our house windows rattled.

6. Las Vegas, Miami Beach, San Diego, and Atlantic City, are the four places she has worked as a bartender.

7. Thomas Farley, the handsome young man, who just took off his trousers, recently escaped from an institution for the mentally ill.

8. Hal wanted to go to medical school, but he does not have the money, and was not offered a scholarship.

9. Joyce reads, a lot of fiction, but I prefer stories that really happened.

10. Because Mary is single, her married friends do not invite her, to their parties.

Collaborative Activity

Editing and Rewriting

Working with a partner, read carefully the short paragraph below and cross out the five misplaced commas. Then, in the space between the lines, insert the ten additional commas needed. Feel free to discuss the rewrite quietly with your partner and refer back to the chapter when necessary.

¹If you want to become a better note-taker you should keep in mind the following hints. ²Most important you should attend class on a regular basis. ³The instructor will probably develop in class, all the main ideas of the course and you want to be there to write the ideas down. ⁴Students often ask "How much, should I write down?" ⁵By paying close attention in class you will probably develop an instinct for the material, that you must write down. ⁶You should record your notes in outline form. ⁷Start main points at the margin indent major supporting details and further indent more subordinate material. ⁸When the speaker moves from one aspect of a topic to another show this shift on your paper, by skipping a line or two. ⁹A last hint but by no means the least is to write down any points your instructor repeats or takes the time, to put on the board.

Creating Sentences

Working with a partner, write sentences that use commas as directed.

1. Write a sentence mentioning three items that can be found in the photo.

    _____

    _____

2. Write two sentences describing how you relax after getting home from school or work. Start the first sentence with *After* or *When*. Start the second sentence with *Next*.

    _____

    _____

3. Write a sentence that tells something about your favorite movie, book, television show, or song. Use the words *which is my favorite movie* (or *book, television show,* or *song*) after the name of the movie, book, television show, or song.

    _____

    _____

4. Write two complete thoughts about a person you know. The first thought should mention something that you like about the person. The second thought should mention something you don't like. Join the two thoughts with *but*.

    _____

    _____

5. Invent a line that Lola might say to Tony. Use the words *Lola said* in the sentence. Then include Tony's reply, using the words *Tony responded.*

    _____

    _____

6. Write a sentence about an important event in your life. Include in your sentence the day, month, and year of the event.

    _____

    _____

Reflective Activity

1. Look at the paragraph on note taking that you revised above. Explain how adding commas has affected the reading of the paragraph.

2. What would writing be like without the comma? How do commas help writing?

3. What is the most difficult comma rule for you to remember and apply? Explain, giving an example.

Review Test 1

Insert commas where needed. In the space provided under each sentence, summarize briefly the rule that explains the use of the comma or commas.

1. After, I fell and fractured my wrist, I decided to sell my skateboard.

   _____

2. She asked her son, "Are you going to church with me tomorrow?"

   _____

3. The weather bureau predicts that sleet, fire, or brimstone will fall on Washington today.

   _____

4. The ignition system in his car, as well as the generator was not working properly.

   _____

5. Tony asked Lola, "Have you ever had nightmares in which some kind of monster was ready to swallow you?"

   _____

6. They attacked their bathroom with Lysol, Comet, and Fantastik.

   _____

7. The pan of bacon fat heating on the stove, burst into flame, and he quickly set a lid on the pan to put out the fire.

   _____

8. Lou's bad cough‚which he had had for almost a week‚began to subside.

_____

9. I wear thick socks while hiking‚but I still return from a trip with blistered feet.

_____

10. When they found pencil shavings in the soup‚the guests decided they were not hungry.

_____

Review Test   2

Insert commas where needed. One sentence does not need commas; mark this sentence *C* for "correct."

1. Some people think school uniforms are a bad idea but I disagree strongly.

2. When I was in high school I did not have a lot of money.

3. I worked in a shoe store every weekend and then I spent my entire paycheck on school clothes.

4. The money enabled me to buy the latest shirts pants and sneakers.

5. Instead of studying or enjoying my friends I spent my time in high school trying to look stylish.

6. I did this I realize now because I thought it would make me popular.

7. If every school required uniforms students would not have to worry so much about clothes.

8. Opponents of school uniforms say that forcing students to wear the same clothes takes away kids' freedom of expression.

9. I on the other hand feel that uniforms free students from the pressure to conform to expensive styles and trends.

10. More important school uniforms allow rich and poor kids to dress equally.

Review Test   3

On separate paper, write six sentences, with each sentence demonstrating one of the six main comma rules.

MASTERY TEST 1 Comma

Add commas where needed. Then refer to the box below and write, in the space provided, the letter of the comma rule that applies in each sentence.

a. Between items in a series	d. Between complete thoughts
b. After introductory material	e. With direct quotations
c. Around interrupters	

_____ 1. The hot dogs that we bought tasted delicious but they reacted later like delayed time bombs.

_____ 2. Because it was the thing to do whenever he talked with the guys Tony pretended he had dated a lot of women.

_____ 3. Angel had no idea what his weight was but Kristina always knew hers.

_____ 4. Lola a good athlete surprised Tony by making forty-six of fifty foul shots.

_____ 5. The child's eyes glowed at the sight of the glittering tree colorful packages and stuffed stockings.

_____ 6. "Before you crack open another walnut" Tony's father warned him "remember that we're going to be eating shortly."

_____ 7. When she got back from the supermarket, she realized she had forgotten to get tofu broccoli and rice.

_____ 8. The old graveyard was filled with vampires werewolves crooked politicians and other monsters.

_____ 9. The problem with you Delilah is that you take criticism personally.

_____ 10. Jerome chose the shortest line at the post office but the woman in front of him suddenly began pulling a number of tiny packages out of her pockets.

SCORE
Number Correct

_____ x 10

_____ %

Comma MASTERY TEST 2

Add commas where needed. Then refer to the box below to write, in the space provided, the letter of the comma rule that applies in each sentence.

a. Between items in a series	d. Between complete thoughts
b. After introductory material	e. With direct quotations
c. Around interrupters	

_____ 1. As soon as Yuji finished the difficult problem he let out a satisfied grunt.

_____ 2. On Saturday if it doesn't rain we plan to take the kids to the ball game.

_____ 3. I don't care if I never see you your family or your vacation pictures again.

_____ 4. Tony quit his part-time job at a local gas station for he was being paid only $5.50 an hour.

_____ 5. "Aunt Flo is so forgetful" my mother observed "that whenever she ties a string around her finger as a reminder, she forgets to look at the string."

_____ 6. The restaurant's special "Italian Omelette" contains eggs tomato mozzarella cheese sausage and salami.

_____ 7. My Aunt Esther loves watching the silly childish antics of the contestants on some game shows.

_____ 8. Although my classes don't begin until ten o'clock I still have trouble getting to the lecture hall on time.

_____ 9. A flock of snow geese their shiny wings flashing in the sun flew above the marshlands.

_____ 10. James brought his own yoga mat to class for he found the mats at the YMCA too thin.

NAME: _____

DATE: _____

MASTERY TEST 3 Comma ✗

Add commas where needed. Then refer to the box below to write, in the space provided, the letter of the one comma rule that applies in each sentence.

a. Between items in a series	d. Between complete thoughts
b. After introductory material	e. With direct quotations
c. Around interrupters	

____d____ 1. Kevin and Tasha took Paul, their son, to see Walt Disney's *Bambi*.

____a____ 2. The film covers the birth of Bambi, the loss of his mother, his escape from a forest fire, and his growth to young fatherhood.

____b____ 3. Just before the film started Kevin decided to get a giant box of Jujyfruits.

____a____ 4. While he was at the refreshment counter, the houselights dimmed, the stage curtains opened, and the movie started.

_____ 5. Kevin hurried back down the dark aisle, almost stumbling, and slipped into the empty aisle seat that he thought was his.

_____ 6. While Kevin popped Jujyfruits into his mouth the woman next to him rested her head on his shoulder.

_____ 7. Kevin's eyes grew accustomed to the dark and he suddenly became aware of an elderly man standing near him in the aisle.

____e____ 8. "Excuse me, Sir", the man said. "You're in my seat."

____a____ 9. Hearing the man's voice, the woman looked up, saw Kevin next to her, and screamed.

_____ 10. "I'm really sorry, Madam," Kevin said. He got up quickly and then saw in front of him waving, and laughing his wife and son.

Dictionary Use MASTERY TEST 1

ITEMS 1–5

Use your dictionary to answer the following questions.

1. How many syllables are in the word *decontaminate?* _____

2. Where is the primary accent in the word *interpretation?* _____

3. In the word *posterity,* the *i* is pronounced like

    a. short *e.*

    b. short *i.*

    c. long *i.*

    d. schwa.

4. In the word *secularize,* the *u* is pronounced like

    a. schwa.

    b. short *a.*

    c. short *u.*

    d. long *u.*

5. In the word *erratic,* the *e* is pronounced like

    a. short *e.*

    b. long *e.*

    c. short *i.*

    d. schwa.

ITEMS 6–10

There are five misspelled words in the following sentence. Cross out each misspelled word and write in the correct spelling in the spaces provided.

The canidate for mayor promised to reduce subway fares by a nickle, to crack down on criminels, and to bring new businesses to the city by ofering tax breaks.

6. _____   8. _____   10. _____

7. _____   9. _____

MASTERY TEST 2 | Dictionary Use

ITEMS **1–5**

Use your dictionary to answer the following questions.

1. How many syllables are in the word *rationalize?*_____

2. Where is the primary accent in the word *dilapidated?*_____

3. In the word *vicarious,* the second *i* is pronounced like

    a. long *e.*

    b. short *i.*

    c. long *i.*

    d. schwa.

4. In the word *cumbersome,* the *o* is pronounced like

    a. schwa.

    b. short *a.*

    c. short *o.*

    d. long *o.*

5. In the word *esoteric,* the second *e* is pronounced like

    a. short *e.*

    b. long *e.*

    c. short *i.*

    d. schwa.

ITEMS **6–10**

There are five misspelled words in the following sentence. Cross out each mis-spelled word and write the correct spelling in the space provided.

My mother's most precious possesion is her collection of crystel animals; she keeps them in a specal cabinet in the dineing room and won't allow anyone to handel them.

6. _____   8. _____   10. _____

7. _____   9. _____

Spelling Improvement

Introductory Activity

See if you can circle the word that is misspelled in each of the following pairs:

akward	*or*	awkward
exercise	*or*	exercize
business	*or*	buisness
worried	*or*	worryed
shamful	*or*	shameful
begining	*or*	beginning
partys	*or*	parties
sandwichs	*or*	sandwiches
heroes	*or*	heros

Answers are on page 573.

Poor spelling often results from bad habits developed in the early school years. With work, such habits can be corrected. If you can write your name without misspelling it, there is no reason why you can't do the same with almost any word in the English language. Following are seven steps you can take to improve your spelling.

Step 1: Using the Dictionary

Get into the habit of using the dictionary. When you write a paper, allow yourself time to look up the spelling of all the words you are unsure about. Do not under-estimate the value of this step just because it is such a simple one. By using the dictionary, you can probably make yourself a 95 percent better speller.

Step 2: Keeping a Personal Spelling List

Keep a list of words you misspell and study those words regularly.

TIP

When you have trouble spelling long words, try to break each word into syllables and see whether you can spell the syllables. For example, *misdemeanor* can be spelled easily if you can hear and spell in turn its four syllables: *mis-de-mean-or*. The word *formidable* can be spelled easily if you hear and spell in turn its four syllables: *for-mi-da-ble*. Remember, then: try to see, hear, and spell long words in terms of their syllables.

Step 3: Mastering Commonly Confused Words

Master the meanings and spellings of the commonly confused words on pages 411–430. Your instructor may assign twenty words for you to study at a time and give you a series of quizzes until you have mastered all the words.

Step 4: Using a Computer's Spell-Checker

Most word-processing programs feature a *spell-checker* that will identify incorrect words and suggest correct spellings. If you are unsure how to use yours, consult the program's "help" function. Spell-checkers are not foolproof; they will fail to catch misused homonyms like the words *your* and *you're*.

Step 5: Understanding Basic Spelling Rules

Explained briefly here are three rules that may improve your spelling. While exceptions sometimes occur, these rules hold true most of the time.

1. Changing y to i.

When a word ends in a consonant plus *y*, change *y* to *i* when you add an ending.

try	+ ed = tried		marry	+ es = marries
worry	+ es = worries		lazy	+ ness = laziness
lucky	+ ly = luckily		silly	+ est = silliest

2. Final silent e.

Drop a final *e* before an ending that starts with a vowel (the vowels are *a, e, i, o,* and *u*).

hope + ing = hoping		sense + ible = sensible
fine + est = finest		hide + ing = hiding

Keep the final *e* before an ending that starts with a consonant.

use + ful = useful		care + less = careless
life + like = lifelike		settle + ment = settlement

3. Doubling a final consonant.

Double the final consonant of a word when all the following are true:

a. The word is one syllable or is accented on the last syllable.
b. The word ends in a single consonant preceded by a single vowel.
c. The ending you are adding starts with a vowel.

sob + ing = sobbing		big + est = biggest
drop + ed = dropped		omit + ed = omitted
admit + ing = admitting		begin + ing = beginning

Practice

1

Combine the following words and endings by applying the three rules above.

1. study + ed = _____
2. advise + ing = _____
3. carry + es = _____
4. stop   + ing = _____
5. terrify + ed = _____
6. compel + ed = _____
7. retire + ing = _____
8. hungry + ly = _____
9. expel + ing = _____
10. judge + es = _____

Step 6: Understanding Plurals

Most words form their plurals by adding *-s* to the singular.

Singular	Plural
blanket	blankets
pencil	pencils
street	streets

Some words, however, form their plurals in special ways, as shown in the rules that follow.

1. **Words ending in *-s, -ss, -z, -x, -sh,* or *-ch* usually form the plural by adding *-es*.**

kiss	kisses	inch	inches
box	boxes	dish	dishes

2. **Words ending in a consonant plus *y* form the plural by changing *y* to *i* and adding *-es*.**

party	parties	county	counties
baby	babies	city	cities

3. **Some words ending in *f* change the *f* to *v* and add *-es* in the plural.**

leaf	leaves	life	lives
wife	wives	yourself	yourselves

4. **Some words ending in *o* form their plurals by adding *-es*.**

potato	potatoes	mosquito	mosquitoes
hero	heroes	tomato	tomatoes

5. **Some words of foreign origin have irregular plurals. When in doubt, check your dictionary.**

antenna	antennae	crisis	crises
criterion	criteria	medium	media

6. **Some words form their plurals by changing letters within the word.**

man	men	foot	feet
tooth	teeth	goose	geese

7. **Combined words (words made up of two or more words) form their plurals by adding -s to the main word.**

brother-in-law	brothers-in-law
passerby	passersby

Complete these sentences by filling in the plural of the word at the left.

grocery 1. I carried six bags of _____ into the house.

town 2. How many _____ did you visit during the tour?

policy 3. The president's new _____ are making many voters angry.

body 4. Because the grave diggers were on strike, _____ piled up in the morgue.

lottery 5. She plays two state _____ in hopes of winning a fortune.

pass 6. Hank caught six _____ in a losing cause.

tragedy 7. That woman has had to endure many _____ in her life.

watch 8. I have found that cheap _____ work better for me than expensive ones.

suit 9. To help himself feel better, he went out and bought two _____.

boss 10. I have not one but two _____ to worry about every day.

Practice

2

Step 7: Mastering a Basic Word List

Make sure you can spell all the words in the following list. They are some of the words used most often in English. Again, your instructor may assign twenty words for you to study at a time and give you a series of quizzes until you have mastered the words.

ability	bargain	daily
absent	beautiful	danger
accident	because	daughter
across	become	death
address	before	decide
advertise	begin	deposit
advice	being	describe
after	believe	different
again	between	direction
against	bottom 40	distance
all right	breathe	doubt
almost	building	dozen
a lot	business	during
although	careful	each
always	careless	early
among	cereal	earth
angry	certain	education
animal	change	either
another	cheap	English
answer 20	chief	enough 80
anxious	children	entrance
apply	church	everything
approve	cigarette	examine
argue	clothing	exercise
around	collect	expect
attempt	color	family
attention	comfortable	flower
awful	company	foreign
awkward	condition	friend
balance	conversation 60	garden

general	middle	pocket
grocery	might	possible
guess	million	potato
happy	minute	president
heard	mistake	pretty
heavy	money	problem
height	month	promise
himself	morning	property
holiday	mountain	psychology
house **100**	much	public
however	needle	question
hundred	neglect	quick
hungry	newspaper	raise
important	noise	ready
instead	none **140**	really
intelligence	nothing	reason
interest	number	receive
interfere	ocean	recognize
kitchen	offer	remember
knowledge	often	repeat **180**
labor	omit	restaurant
language	only	ridiculous
laugh	operate	said
leave	opportunity	same
length	original	sandwich
lesson	ought	send
letter	pain	sentence
listen	paper	several
loneliness	pencil	shoes
making **120**	people	should
marry	perfect	since
match	period	sleep
matter	personal	smoke
measure	picture	something
medicine	place **160**	soul

started	through	usual
state	ticket	value
straight	tired	vegetable
street	today	view
strong **200**	together	visitor
student	tomorrow	voice
studying	tongue	warning
success	tonight	watch
suffer	touch	welcome
surprise	travel **220**	window
teach	truly	would
telephone	understand	writing
theory	unity	written
thought	until	year
thousand	upon	yesterday **240**

Can you find the sentence-skills mistake in the sign pictured here? On a separate piece of paper, write a paragraph on what you think of establishments that present signs filled with errors.

Review Test

Use the three spelling rules to spell the following words.

1. cry + es = _____

2. believe + able = _____

3. bury + ed = _____

4. date + ing = _____

5. lonely + est = _____

6. large + er = _____

7. skim + ed = _____

8. rare + ly = _____

Circle the correctly spelled plural in each pair.

9. beliefs   believs

10. churchs   churches

11. bullys   bullies

12. countries   countrys

13. womans   women

14. potatos   potatoes

Circle the correctly spelled word (from the basic word list) in each pair.

15. foreign   foriegn

16. condicion   condition

17. restarant   restaurant

18. opportunity   oportunity

19. entrance   enterance

20. surprise   surprize

NAME: _____

DATE: _____

MASTERY TEST 1 | Spelling Improvement

ITEMS 1–8

Use the three spelling rules to spell the following words.

1. debate + able = _____
2. run + ing = _____
3. thorny + est = _____
4. woe + ful = _____
5. swim + er = _____
6. happy + ly = _____
7. hate + ful = _____
8. infer + ed = _____

ITEMS 9–14

Circle the correctly spelled plural in each pair.

9. knifes   knives   12. stories   storys
10. wishes   wishs   13. heros   heroes
11. decoys   decoies   14. ourselfs   ourselves

ITEMS 15–20

Circle the correctly spelled word (from the basic word list on pages 398–400) in each pair.

15. possible   possable   18. success   sucess
16. exercize   exercise   19. rediculous   ridiculous
17. receive   recieve   20. acident   accident

SECTION 5: WORD USE

know	to understand
no	a negative

I never *know* who might drop in even though *no* one is expected.

Fill in the blanks: When that spoiled boy's parents say ____no____ to him, we all ____know____ a temper tantrum is likely to result.

Write sentences using *know* and *no*.

_____

_____

pair	a set of two
pear	a fruit

The dessert consisted of a *pair* of thin biscuits topped with vanilla ice cream and poached *pear* halves.

Fill in the blanks: The grove of ____pear____ trees is one of the places where the ____pair____ of bear cubs have been playing.

Write sentences using *pair* and *pear*.

_____

_____

| passed | went by; succeeded in; handed to |
| past | by, as in "I drove past the house"; a time before the present |

After Emma *passed* the driver's test, she drove *past* all her friends' houses and honked the horn.

Fill in the blanks: In her __past__ jobs, Nadia had __passed__ up several opportunities for promotion because she did not want to seem aggressive.

Write sentences using *passed* and *past.*

_____

_____

| peace | calm |
| piece | a part |

The *peace* of the little town was shattered when a *piece* of a human body was found in the town dump.

Fill in the blanks: The judge promised to give the troublemaker more than just a __piece__ of his mind if the boy ever disturbed the __peace__ again.

Write sentences using *peace* and *piece.*

_____

_____

plain	simple
plane	aircraft

The *plain* box contained a very expensive model *plane* kit.

Fill in the blanks: That ___plain___-looking man boarding the
___plane___ is actually a famous movie director.

Write sentences using *plain* and *plane*.

_____

_____

principal	main; a person in charge of a school; amount of money borrowed
principle	a law or standard

My *principal* goal in child rearing is to give my daughter strong *principles* to live by.

Fill in the blanks: The school ___principal___ defended the school's
___principle___ regarding a dress code for students.

Write sentences using *principal* and *principle*.

_____

_____

TIP It might help to remember that the *le* in *principle* is also in *rule*—the meaning of *principle*.

right	correct; opposite of *left;* privilege
write	**what you do in English**

It is my *right* to refuse to *write* my name on your petition.

Fill in the blanks: Ellen wanted to ___write___ and thank Steve for his flowers, but she didn't think it ___right___ to keep leading him on.

Write sentences using *right* and *write.*

_____

_____

than	used in comparisons
then	at that time

I glared angrily at my boss, and *then* I told him our problems were more serious *than* he suspected.

Fill in the blanks: I went to the front porch to get my newspaper, and ___then___ I made my breakfast. The news on the front page was much more cheerful ___than___ it had been the day before.

Write sentences using *than* and *then.*

_____

_____

TIP It might help to remember that *then* is also a time signal.

| a | | Both *a* and *an* are used before other words to mean, approximately, *one*. |
| an | | |

Generally you should use *an* before words starting with a vowel (*a, e, i, o, u*):

   an absence   an exhibit   an idol   an offer   an upgrade

Generally you should use *a* before words starting with a consonant (all other letters):

   a pen   a ride   a digital clock   a movie   a neighbor

Fill in the blanks: Lola bought her mother _____*an*_____ orchid and _____*a*_____ slinky nightgown for her birthday.

Write sentences using *a* and *an*.

_____

_____

| accept | receive; agree to |
| except | exclude; but |

   If I *accept* your advice, I'll lose all my friends *except* you.

Fill in the blanks: _____ for one detail, my client is willing to _____ this offer.

Write sentences using *accept* and *except.*

_____

_____

> advice   **noun meaning** *an opinion*
> advise   **verb meaning** *to counsel, to give advice*

Jake never listened to his parents' *advice,* and he ended up listening to a cop *advise* him of his rights.

Fill in the blanks: Nelson's doctor said, "I _____ you to follow my diet rather than take the _____ of the minister who promised you could lose weight through prayer."

Write sentences using *advice* and *advise.*

_____

_____

> affect   **verb meaning** *to influence*
> effect   **verb meaning** *to bring about something;*
>   **noun meaning** *result*

My sister Nicole cries for *effect,* but my parents caught on and her act no longer *affects* them.

Fill in the blanks: The loud music began to _____ my hearing, creating a high-pitched ringing _____ in my ears.

Write sentences using *affect* and *effect.*

_____

_____

among	implies three or more
between	implies only two

We selfishly divided the box of candy *between* the two of us rather than *among* all the members of the family.

Fill in the blanks: _____ the twenty-five people on the camping trip, arguments developed only _____ the two counselors.

Write sentences using *among* and *between.*

_____

_____

beside	along the side of
besides	in addition to

Jamal sat *beside* Teresa. *Besides* them, there were four thousand other people at the Beyonce show.

Fill in the blanks: I love this class; _____ the fact that the course has thought-provoking content, I sit _____ a Brad Pitt look-alike.

Write sentences using *beside* and *besides.*

_____

_____

can	refers to the ability to do something
may	refers to permission or possibility

If you *can* work overtime on Saturday, you *may* take Monday off.

Fill in the blanks: When she _____ speak English fluently, she _____ be eligible for that job.

Write sentences using *can* and *may.*

_____

_____

clothes	articles of dress
cloths	pieces of fabric

I tore up some old *clothes* to use as polishing *cloths.*

Fill in the blanks: I keep some _____ next to me to wipe up any food spills before they reach the baby's _____.

Write sentences using *clothes* and *cloths.*

_____

_____

desert	noun meaning *a stretch of dry land*; verb meaning to *abandon one's post or duty*
dessert	noun meaning *last part of a meal*

Don't *desert* us now; order a sinful *dessert* along with us.

Fill in the blanks: When it's time to order _____, that man's appetite will never _____ him.

Write sentences using *desert* and *dessert.*

_____

_____

can't hardly couldn't hardly	**Incorrect!** Use *can hardly* or *could hardly.*

can

Small store owners ~~can't~~ hardly afford to offer large discounts.

Correct the following sentences.

1. I can't hardly understand why Nelson would cut class when he's madly in love with the instructor.

2. You can't hardly imagine how I felt when I knocked over my aunt's favorite plant.

3. You couldn't hardly see last night because of the heavy fog.

could of must of should of would of	**Incorrect!** Use *could have, must have, should have, would have.*

have

I should ~~of~~ applied for a loan when my credit was good.

Correct the following sentences.

1. Anita must of gone home from work early.

2. I should of started reading the textbook early in the semester.

3. If the game had been canceled, they would of been very disappointed.

4. If Shirelle had wanted to, she could of come with us.

irregardless	**Incorrect!** Use *regardless.*

Regardless

~~Irregardless~~ of what anyone says, he will not change his mind.

Correct the following sentences.

1. They decided to buy the house irregardless of the price.

2. That company insures people irregardless of their age or state of health.

3. Irregardless of the risk, I started mountain climbing as a hobby.

Review Test 1

These sentences check your understanding of *its, it's; there, their, they're; to, too, two;* and *your, you're.* Underline the correct word in the parentheses. Rather than guess, look back at the explanations of the words when necessary.

1. Some stores will accept (your, you're) credit card but not (your, you're) money.

2. I know (its, it's) late, but (its, it's) important to get this job done properly.

3. (There, Their, They're) is a good baseball game down at the playground, but (there, their, they're) (to, too, two) busy to walk down (there, their, they're).

4. (Its, It's) been two hours since I put the turkey in the oven, but (its, it's) still not ready.

5. (There, Their, They're) going to be away for (to, too, two) weeks and want me to go over to (there, their, they're) yard to water (there, their, they're) rosebushes.

6. (Your, You're) going to have to do a better job on (your, you're) final exam if you expect to pass the course.

7. That issue is (to, too, two) hot for any politician (to, too, two) handle.

8. If (your, you're) hoping to get good grades on (your, you're) essay tests, you need to improve (your, you're) handwriting.

9. (There, Their, They're) planning to trade in (there, their, they're) old car for a new one before taking (there, their, they're) vacation.

10. (Your, You're) going to have to put aside individual differences and play together for the benefit of (your, you're) team.

Review Test 2

The sentences that follow check your understanding of a variety of commonly confused words. Underline the correct word in the parentheses. Rather than guess, look back at the explanations of the words when necessary.

1. I try to get (through, threw) each day without shopping for shoes. Once I (through, threw) away my latest magazines because their tempting shoe ads were (affecting, effecting) my resolve.

2. We weren't sure (whether, weather) or not a storm was brewing until several hours had passed. (Then, Than) the air became (quiet, quite), clouds formed, and we (knew, new) enough to run indoors.

3. (Being that, Since) "Stormy (Weather, Whether)" is her favorite song, I (should of, should have) gotten her an album with that song on it.

4. Take my (advice, advise) and hurry down (to, too, two) the radio station. You'll get a (pair, pear) of free tickets to the rock concert.

5. For Lola the (principal, principle) (course, coarse) of the meal—a (desert, dessert) of French vanilla ice cream and blueberry pie—was yet (to, too, two) come.

6. (Its, It's) obvious why people are not eating the cheese; (there, their, they're) frightened by (its, it's) unusual smell.

7. The first (course, coarse) of the meal was soup. Its (principal, principle) ingredient was onion, to which I'm allergic. Trying to be polite, I ate one mouthful, but (than, then) I began to sneeze uncontrollably.

8. As he (passed, past) by the church, he (though, thought) of the Sunday mornings he had spent (there, their, they're) in the (passed, past).

9. The night after I watched the chiller movie, I dreamed that (a, an) gigantic (hole, whole) opened up in the earth, swallowed a whole city, and (than, then) tried to swallow me, (to, too, two).

10. "I'm going to let you be my (knew, new) woman," the man declared. "(Your, You're) my (peace, piece) of property from now on."

   "(Whose, Who's) messed up (your, you're) head?" the woman replied. "I can't believe I (hear, here) you (right, write). (Where, Wear) are you at? I think you have been (affected, effected) by the sun."

Review Test 3

On separate paper, write short sentences using the ten words shown below.

there	then	you're	affect	who's
past	advise	too (meaning *also*)	its	break

NAME: _____

DATE: _____

MASTERY TEST 1 | Commonly Confused Words

Choose the correct words in each sentence and write them in the spaces provided.

_____

_____

1. Last year the (hole, whole) publishing industry seemed to concentrate on turning out (knew, new) romantic novels.

_____

2. We drove out into the (dessert, desert) (to, too, two) test our dune buggies.

_____

3. Joseph could not (know, no) that it would be Carmella who would (break, brake) his heart.

_____

4. My dog lost (its, it's) tail after being run over by a truck that had lost its (brakes, breaks).

_____

5. (Irregardless, Regardless) of what her co-workers think, Susan always wears plain (clothes, cloths) to work.

_____

6. Pete (could of, could have) used the money, but he refused to (accept, except) the check his parents offered him.

_____

7. Morris can't stand to (hear, here) advice. He lives by the (principal, principle), "If I make my own decisions, I have only myself to praise or blame."

_____

8. Kevin and Judy have to make (there, their, they're) handwriting neater and more legible if (there, their, they're) after good grades.

_____

9. Just (among, between) us, I'd advise you not to take Dear Abby's (advice, advise) as gospel.

_____

10. That lion over (there, their, they're) clawed at the attendant cleaning (it's, its) cage.

Inflated Words	Simpler Words
component	part
delineate	describe
facilitate	help
finalize	finish
initiate	begin
manifested	shown
subsequent to	after
to endeavor	to try
transmit	send

Cross out the two pretentious words in each sentence. Then substitute clear, simple language for the pretentious words.

Practice

4

EXAMPLE

Sally was ~~terminated~~ from her ~~employment~~.

Sally was fired from her job.

1. My television receiver is not operative.

   _____

2. We made an expedition to the mall to see the new fall apparel.

   _____

3. José indicated an aversion to fish.

   _____

4. The fans expressed their displeasure when the pitcher threw the ball erratically.

   _____

5. How long have you resided in that municipality?

   _____

Wordiness

Wordiness—using more words than necessary to express a meaning—is often a sign of lazy or careless writing. Your readers may resent the extra time and energy they must spend when you have not done the work needed to make your writing direct and concise.

Following is a list of some wordy expressions that could be reduced to single words.

www.mhhe.com/langan

Wordy Form	Short Form
a large number of	many
a period of a week	a week
arrive at an agreement	agree
at an earlier point in time	before
at the present time	now
big in size	big
due to the fact that	because
during the time that	while
five in number	five
for the reason that	because
good benefit	benefit
in every instance	always
in my opinion	I think
in the event that	if
in the near future	soon
in this day and age	today
is able to	can
large in size	large
plan ahead for the future	plan
postponed until later	postponed
red in color	red
return back	return

Here are examples of wordy sentences:

At this point in time in our country, the amount of violence seems to be increasing every day.

I called to the children repeatedly to get their attention, but my shouts did not get any response from them.

Omitting needless words improves these sentences:

Violence is increasing in our country.

I called to the children repeatedly, but they didn't respond.

Rewrite the following sentences, omitting needless words.

EXAMPLE

Starting as of the month of June, I will be working at the store on a full-time basis.

As of June, I will be working at the store full time.

1. Because of the fact that it was raining, I didn't go shopping.

   _____

2. As far as I am concerned, in my opinion I do not feel that prostitution should be legalized.

   _____

3. Please do not hesitate to telephone me if you would like me to come into your office for an interview.

   _____

4. During the time that I was sick and out of school, I missed a total of three math tests.

   _____

5. Well-paying jobs are all too few and far between unless a person has a high degree of training.

   _____

Review Test 1

Certain words are italicized in the following sentences. In the space provided, identify whether the words are slang (*S*), clichés (*C*), or pretentious words (*PW*). Then replace them with more effective words.

_____ 1. If the boss starts *putting heat* on me again, I'm going to quit.

            _____

_____ 2. Because of the rain, I wore a jacket that *has seen better days.*

            _____

_____ 3. Ted won't help us unless we offer *a monetary reward.*

            _____

_____ 4. When my younger brother did not get home from the party until 2 A.M., my mother decided *to put her foot down.*

_____

_____ 5. My upset stomach was *alleviated* by the antacid.

_____

_____ 6. The vacation spot was a *total ripoff;* the weather and the food were both *the pits.*

_____

_____ 7. Phan *saw the error of his ways* and began to work harder.

_____

_____ 8. I needed *a respite from my exertions* after I finished texting each and every one of my friends.

_____

_____ 9. I *jumped for joy* when I heard about the promotion.

_____

_____ 10. *You could have wiped me off the floor* when I learned I had earned a full scholarship.

_____

Review Test 2

Rewrite the following sentences, omitting needless words.

1. At this point in time, I cannot say with any degree of certainty that I am planning to participate in the blood drive.

_____

_____

2. Due to the fact that there was no consensus of opinion, the committee agreed that it should meet again.

_____

_____

Passage B

[1]Studies have found that people have a psychological need for plants. [2]People who grew up in urban areas one survey revealed often mentioned the presence or absence of lawns in their neighborhood. [3]One person observed "I realized how much I missed lawns and trees after living in a city where concrete covered everything." [4]Unfortunately the city is a difficult environment for plants. [5]The soil of the city is covered mostly with buildings and pavements so there is little space for plants to grow. [6]Plants that are present are often hurt by haze smog and air pollution. [7]Some plants are more sensitive to pollution than others; snapdragons for example do poorly in polluted air. [8]When planners choose what kind of plants to place in urban areas they must consider the plants' chances for survival under the difficult growing conditions of city streets.

Sentences with missing commas (write down the number of a sentence as many times as it contains comma mistakes):

_____ _____ _____ _____ _____

_____ _____ _____ _____ _____

NAME: _____

DATE: _____

TEST 12 ## Commonly Confused Words

Mistakes in each passage: 10

Passage A

[1]Recently, I was driving across town in heavy city traffic. [2]Cars followed one another bumper-to-bumper, and their were bicyclists and pedestrians darting threw the streets. [3]Beside the heavy traffic, it had begun to rain, making the traffic situation even worse. [4]I was driving cautiously, keeping ten feet or so from the rear of the car in front of me. [5]Than, in my rearview mirror, I noticed the woman behind me. [6]Her car was so close our bumpers were almost locked. [7]Her face was red and angry, and she tapped impatiently on her steering wheel. [8]Suddenly, she saw a five-second brake in the traffic. [9]She past me with a roar and squeezed in ahead of me. [10]I though angrily, "Your a complete idiot!" and honked my horn. [11]She honked back at me and lifted her hand in an obscene gesture. [12]I am a little ashamed at the affect this had on me—I was so enraged I wanted to drag her out of her car and punch her. [13]It took me more than an hour to calm down completely and except the fact that the incident had been a very minor one.

Sentences with commonly confused words (write down the number of a sentence twice if it contains two commonly confused words):

_____ _____ _____ _____ _____

_____ _____ _____ _____ _____

Passage B

[1]If at all possible, try to take you're summer vacation any time accept during the summer. [2]First, by scheduling your vacation at another time of the year, you will avoid the crowds. [3]You will not have to fight the traffic around resort areas or drive passed dozens of motels with "No Vacancy" signs. [4]Beaches and campsites will be quite, to. [5]By vacationing out of season, you will also see many areas at there most beautiful, without the bother of summer's heat, thunderstorms, and insects. [6]Weather you go in spring or fall, you can travel by car without feeling stuck to your seat or to exhausted to explore the city or park. [7]Finally, an off-season trip can save you money. [8]Before and after the summer, prices at resorts drop, for fewer people are demanding reservations. [9]Its possible to stay too weeks for the price of one; or you might stay in a luxury hotel you might not otherwise be able to afford.

Sentences with commonly confused words (write down the number of a sentence twice if it contains two commonly confused words):

_____   _____   _____   _____   _____

_____   _____   _____   _____   _____

Combined Editing Tests

Psychologists have concluded that there are significant differences in being an only, oldest, middle, or youngest child. Which of these are you, and how did it influence the way you were brought up? Jot down the advantages and disadvantages that come to mind. Use the most important ideas on your list to develop a paragraph on how you think your position in your family affected you.

- Print out your work at the end of every session. Then you will have not only your most recent draft to work on away from the computer but also yet another backup in case something should happen to your disks.

- Work in single spacing so that you can see as much of your writing on the screen at one time as possible. Just before you print out your work, change to double spacing.

- Before making major changes in a paper, create a new version using the "Save As" option rather than the "Save" option. For example, if your original file is titled "Once Upon a Time," call the new file "Once Upon a Time V.2." Then make all your changes in that new file. If you decide you don't want those changes, you can go back and use your original file. To keep your files organized, you can also create a folder to store all versions of "Once Upon a Time" or all papers related to a certain subject.

Using a Computer at Each Stage of the Writing Process

Following are some ways to use a computer in your writing.

Prewriting

If you're a fast typist, many kinds of prewriting will go well on the computer. With freewriting in particular, you can get ideas onto the screen almost as quickly as they occur to you. A passing thought that could be productive is not likely to get lost. You may even find it helpful, when freewriting, to dim the screen of your monitor so that you can't see what you're typing. If you temporarily can't see the screen, you won't have to worry about grammar or spelling or typing errors (all of which do not matter in prewriting); instead, you can concentrate on getting down as many ideas and details as possible about your subject.

After any initial freewriting, questioning, and list making on a computer, it's often very helpful to print out a hard copy of what you've done. With a clean printout in front of you, you'll be able to see everything at once and revise and expand your work with handwritten comments in the margins of the paper.

Word processing also makes it easy for you to experiment with the wording of the point of your paper. You can try a number of versions in a short time. After you have decided on the version that works best, you can easily delete the other versions—or simply move them to a temporary "leftover" section at the end of the paper.

Preparing a Scratch Outline

If you have prepared a list of items during prewriting, you may be able to turn that list into an outline right on the screen. Delete the ideas you feel should not be in your paper (saving them at the end of the file in case you change your mind), and add any new ideas that occur to you. Then use the cut and paste functions to shuffle the supporting ideas around until you find the best order for your paper.

Writing Your First Draft

Like many writers, you may want to write out your first draft by hand and then type it into the computer for revision. Even as you type your handwritten draft, you may find yourself making some changes and improvements. And once you have a draft on the screen, or printed out, you will find it much easier to revise than a handwritten one.

If you feel comfortable composing directly on the screen, you can benefit from the computer's special features. For example, if you have written an anecdote in your freewriting that you plan to use in your paper, simply copy the story from your freewriting file and insert it where it fits in your paper. You can refine it then or later. Or if you discover while typing that a sentence is out of place, cut it out from where it is and paste it wherever you wish. And if while writing you realize that an earlier sentence can be expanded, just move your cursor back to that point and type in the added material.

Revising

It is during revision that the virtues of a computer really shine. All substituting, adding, deleting, and rearranging can be done easily within an existing file. All changes instantly take their proper places within the paper, not scribbled above the line or squeezed into the margin. You can concentrate on each change you want to make, because you never have to type from scratch or work on a messy draft. You can carefully go through your paper to check that all your supporting evidence is relevant and to add new support as needed here and there. Anything you decide to eliminate can be deleted in a keystroke. Anything you add can be inserted precisely where you choose. If you change your mind, all you have to do is delete or cut and paste. Then you can sweep through the paper, focusing on other changes, such as improving word choice, increasing sentence variety, eliminating wordiness, and so on.

If you are like many students, you will find it convenient to print out a hard copy of your file at various points throughout the revision. You can then revise in longhand—adding, crossing out, and indicating changes—and later quickly make these changes in the document.

Editing and Proofreading

A computer is a great tool for editing and proofreading. Instead of crossing out mistakes or using correction fluid or tape—or rewriting an entire paper to correct numerous errors—you can make all necessary changes directly to your work file. If you find editing or proofreading on the screen hard on your eyes, print out a copy. Mark any corrections on that copy, and then transfer them to your file.

If the word-processing software you're using includes spelling and grammar checks, by all means use them. The spell-check function tells you when a word is not in the computer's dictionary. Keep in mind, however, that the spell-checker cannot tell you how to spell a name correctly or when you have mistakenly used, for example, *their* instead of *there*. To a spell-checker, *Thank ewe four the compliment* is as correct as *Thank you for the compliment.* Also, use the grammar checker with caution. Any errors it doesn't uncover are still your responsibility, and it may signal possible errors that don't exist in your paper.

A freshly printed paper, with its clean appearance and handsome formatting, looks so good that you may feel it is in better shape than it really is. Do not be fooled by your paper's appearance. Take sufficient time to review your grammar, punctuation, and spelling carefully.

Even after you hand in your paper, save the computer file. Your instructor may ask you to do some revising, and then the file will save you from having to type the paper from scratch.

Parts of Speech

Words—the building blocks of sentences—can be divided into eight parts of speech. *Parts of speech* are classifications of words according to their meaning and use in a sentence.

This chapter will explain the eight parts of speech:

nouns	prepositions	conjunctions
pronouns	adjectives	interjections
verbs	adverbs	

Nouns

A *noun* is a word that is used to name something: a person, a place, an object, or an idea. Here are some examples of nouns:

Nouns			
woman	city	pancake	freedom
Alice Walker	street	diamond	possibility
Steve Martin	Chicago	Corvette	mystery

Most nouns begin with a lowercase letter and are known as *common nouns*. These nouns name general things. Some nouns, however, begin with a capital letter. They are called *proper nouns*. While a common noun refers to a person or thing in general, a proper noun names someone or something specific. For example, *woman* is a common noun—it doesn't name a particular woman. On the other hand, *Alice Walker* is a proper noun because it names a specific woman.

Insert any appropriate noun into each of the following blanks.

Practice

1

1. The shoplifter stole a(n) _____ from the department store.

2. _____ threw the football to me.

3. Tiny messages were scrawled on the _____.

4. A _____ crashed through the window.

5. Give the _____ to Keiko.

Singular and Plural Nouns

A *singular noun* names one person, place, object, or idea. A *plural noun* refers to two or more persons, places, objects, or ideas. Most singular nouns can be made plural with the addition of an *s*.

Some nouns, like *box*, have irregular plurals. You can check the plural of nouns you think may be irregular by looking up the singular form in a dictionary.

Singular and Plural Nouns

Singular	Plural
goat	goats
alley	alleys
friend	friends
truth	truths
box	boxes

For more information on nouns, see "Subjects and Verbs," pages 66–78.

Underline the three nouns in the following sentences. Some are singular, and some are plural.

Practice

2

1. Two bats swooped over the heads of the frightened children.

2. The artist has purple paint on her sleeve.

3. The lost dog has fleas and a broken leg.

4. Tiffany does her homework in green ink.

5. Some farmers plant seeds by moonlight.

Pronouns

A *pronoun* is a word that stands for a noun. Pronouns eliminate the need for constant repetition. Look at the following sentences:

> The phone rang, and Malik answered the phone.

> Lisa met Lisa's friends at the ice-skating rink. Lisa meets Lisa's friends there every Saturday.

> The waiter rushed over to the new customers. The new customers asked the waiter for menus and coffee.

Notice how much clearer and smoother these sentences sound with pronouns.

> The phone rang, and Malik answered *it*. (The pronoun *it* is used to replace the word *phone*.)

> Lisa met *her* friends at the ice-skating rink. *She* meets *them* there every Saturday. (The pronoun *her* is used to replace the word *Lisa's*. The pronoun *she* replaces *Lisa*. The pronoun *them* replaces the words *Lisa's friends*.)

> The waiter rushed over to the new customers. *They* asked *him* for menus and coffee. (The pronoun *they* is used to replace the words *the new customers*. The pronoun *him* replaces the words *the waiter*.)

Following is a list of commonly used pronouns known as *personal pronouns:*

Personal Pronouns

I	you	he	she	it	we	they
me	your	him	her	its	us	them
my	yours	his	hers		our	their

Fill in each blank with the appropriate personal pronoun.

1. André feeds his pet lizard every day before school. _____ also
    gives _____ flies in the afternoon.

2. The reporter interviewed the striking workers. _____ told
    _____ about their demand for higher wages and longer breaks.

3. Students should save all returned tests. _____ should also keep
    _____ review sheets.

4. The pilot announced that we would fly through some air pockets. _____
    said that we should be past _____ soon.

5. Adolfo returned the calculator to Sheila last Friday. But Sheila insists that
    _____ never got _____ back.

There are several types of pronouns. For convenient reference, they are
described briefly in the box below.

Types of Pronouns

Personal pronouns can act in a sentence as subjects, objects, or possessives.

    Singular: **I, me, my, mine, you, your, yours, he, him, his, she, her, hers, it, its**

    Plural: **we, us, our, ours, you, your, yours, they, them, their, theirs**

Relative pronouns refer to someone or something already mentioned in the
sentence.

        who, whose, whom, which, that

Interrogative pronouns are used to ask questions.

        who, whose, whom, which, what

Demonstrative pronouns are used to point out particular persons or things.

        this, that, these, those

Note: Do not use *them* (as in *them* shoes), *this here, that there, these here,* or
those there to point out.

continued

Reflexive pronouns are those that end in *-self* or *-selves*. A reflexive pronoun is used as the object of a verb (as in *Cary cut **herself***) or the object of a preposition (as in *Jack sent a birthday card to **himself***) when the subject of the verb is the same as the object.

   Singular: **myself, yourself, himself, herself, itself**

   Plural: **ourselves, yourselves, themselves**

Intensive pronouns have exactly the same forms as reflexive pronouns. The difference is in how they are used. Intensive pronouns are used to add emphasis. (*I **myself** will need to read the contract before I sign it.*)

Indefinite pronouns do not refer to a particular person or thing.

      each, either, everyone, nothing, both, several, all, any, most, none

Reciprocal pronouns express shared actions or feelings.

      each other, one another

For more information on pronouns, see "Pronoun Types," pages 216–230.

Verbs

Every complete sentence must contain at least one verb. There are two types of verbs: action verbs and linking verbs.

Action Verbs

An *action verb* tells what is being done in a sentence. For example, look at the following sentences:

   Mr. Jensen *swatted* at the bee with his hand.

   Rainwater *poured* into the storm sewer.

   The children *chanted* the words to the song.

In these sentences, the verbs are *swatted, poured*, and *chanted*. These words are all action verbs; they tell what is happening in each sentence.

For more about action verbs, see "Subjects and Verbs," pages 68–70.

Insert an appropriate word in each blank. That word will be an action verb; it will tell what is happening in the sentence.

Practice

4

1. The surgeon _____ through the first layer of skin.

2. The animals in the cage _____ all day.

3. An elderly woman on the street _____ me for directions.

4. The boy next door _____ our lawn every other week.

5. Our instructor _____ our papers over the weekend.

Linking Verbs

Some verbs are *linking verbs.* These verbs link (or join) a noun to something that is said about it. For example, look at the following sentence:

The clouds *are* steel-gray.

In this sentence, *are* is a linking verb. It joins the noun *clouds* to words that describe it: *steel-gray.*

Other common linking verbs include *am, is, was, were, look, feel, sound, appear, seem,* and *become.* For more about linking verbs, see "Subjects and Verbs," pages 68–70.

In each blank, insert one of the following linking verbs: *am, feel, is, look, were.* Use each linking verb once.

Practice

5

1. The important papers _____ in a desk drawer.

2. I _____ anxious to get my test back.

3. The bananas _____ ripe.

4. The grocery store _____ open until 11 P.M.

5. Whenever I _____ angry, I go off by myself to calm down.

Helping Verbs

Sometimes the verb of a sentence consists of more than one word. In these cases, the main verb will be joined by one or more *helping verbs.* Look at the following sentence:

The basketball team *will be leaving* for the game at six o'clock.

In this sentence, the main verb is *leaving.* The helping verbs are *will* and *be.*

Other helping verbs include *do, has, have, may, would, can, must, could,* and *should.* For more information about helping verbs, see "Subjects and Verbs," pages 71–72, and "Irregular Verbs," pages 156–170.

In each blank, insert one of the following helping verbs: *does, must, should, could, has been.* Use each helping verb once.

1. You _____ start writing your paper this weekend.

2. The victim _____ describe her attacker in great detail.

3. You _____ rinse the dishes before putting them into the dishwasher.

4. My neighbor _____ arrested for drunk driving.

5. The bus driver _____ not make any extra stops.

Prepositions

A *preposition* is a word that connects a noun or a pronoun to another word in the sentence. For example, look at the following sentence:

A man *in* the bus was snoring loudly.

In is a preposition. It connects the noun *bus* to *man*. Here is a list of common prepositions:

Prepositions				
about	before	down	like	to
above	behind	during	of	toward
across	below	except	off	under
after	beneath	for	on	up
among	beside	from	over	with
around	between	in	since	without
at	by	into	through	

The noun or pronoun that a preposition connects to another word in the sentence is called the *object* of the preposition. A group of words beginning with a preposition and ending with its object is called a *prepositional phrase.* The words *in the bus,* for example, are a prepositional phrase.

Now read the following sentences and explanations.

An ant was crawling *up the teacher's leg*.

The noun *leg* is the object of the preposition *up*. *Up* connects *leg* with the word *crawling*. The prepositional phrase *up the teacher's leg* describes *crawling*. It tells just where the ant was crawling.

The man *with the black mustache* left the restaurant quickly.

The noun *mustache* is the object of the preposition *with*. The prepositional phrase *with the black mustache* describes the word *man*. It tells us exactly which man left the restaurant quickly.

The plant *on the windowsill* was a present *from my mother*.

The noun *windowsill* is the object of the preposition *on*. The prepositional phrase *on the windowsill* describes the word *plant*. It describes exactly which plant was a present.

There is a second prepositional phrase in this sentence. The preposition is *from*, and its object is *mother*. The prepositional phrase *from my mother* explains *present*. It tells who gave the present. For more about prepositions, see "Subjects and Verbs," pages 70–71, and "Sentence Variety II," pages 267–283.

In each blank, insert one of the following prepositions: *of, by, with, in, without*. Use each preposition once.

1. The letter from his girlfriend had been sprayed _____ perfume.

2. The weed killer quickly killed the dandelions _____ our lawn.

3. _____ giving any notice, the tenant moved out of the apartment.

4. Donald hungrily ate three scoops _____ ice cream and an order of french fries.

5. The crates _____ the door contain glass bottles and newspapers.

Adjectives

An *adjective* is a word that describes a noun (the name of a person, place, or thing). Look at the following sentence.

The dog lay down on a mat in front of the fireplace.

Now look at this sentence when adjectives have been inserted.

The *shaggy* dog lay down on a *worn* mat in front of the fireplace.

The adjective *shaggy* describes the noun *dog;* the adjective *worn* describes the noun *mat.* Adjectives add spice to our writing. They also help us to identify particular people, places, or things.

Adjectives can be found in two places:

1. An adjective may come before the word it describes (a *damp* night, the *moldy* bread, a *striped* umbrella).

2. An adjective that describes the subject of a sentence may come after a linking verb. The linking verb may be a form of the verb *be* (he *is* **furious**, I *am* **exhausted**, they are **hungry**). Other linking verbs include *feel, look, sound, smell, taste, appear, seem,* and *become* (the soup *tastes* **salty**, your hands *feel* **dry**, the dog *seems* **lost**).

> **TIP** The words *a, an,* and *the* (called *articles*) are generally classified as adjectives.

For more information on adjectives, see "Adjectives and Adverbs," pages 231–239.

Practice

8

Write any appropriate adjective in each blank.

1. The _____ pizza was eaten greedily by the _____ teenagers.

2. Melissa gave away the sofa because it was _____ and _____.

3. Although the alley is _____ and _____, Jian often takes it as a shortcut home.

4. The restaurant throws away lettuce that is _____ and tomatoes that are _____.

5. When I woke up in the morning, I had a(n) _____ fever and a(n) _____ throat.

Adverbs

An *adverb* is a word that describes a verb, an adjective, or another adverb. Many adverbs end in the letters *-ly*. Look at the following sentence:

> The canary sang in the pet store window as the shoppers greeted each other.

Now look at this sentence after adverbs have been inserted.

> The canary sang *softly* in the pet store window as the shoppers *loudly* greeted each other.

The adverbs add details to the sentence. They also allow the reader to contrast the singing of the canary and the noise the shoppers are making.

Look at the following sentences and the explanations of how adverbs are used in each case.

> The chef yelled **angrily** at the young waiter.
> (The adverb *angrily* describes the verb *yelled*.)

> My mother has an **extremely** busy schedule on Tuesdays.
> (The adverb *extremely* describes the adjective *busy*.)

> The sick man spoke **very** faintly to his loyal nurse.
> (The adverb *very* describes the adverb *faintly*.)

Some adverbs do not end in *-ly*. Examples include *very, often, never, always,* and *well*.

For more information on adverbs, see "Adjectives and Adverbs," pages 231–239.

Fill in each blank with any appropriate adverb.

Practice

9

1. The water in the pot boiled _____.

2. Carla _____ drove the car through _____ moving traffic.

3. The telephone operator spoke _____ to the young child.

4. The game show contestant waved _____ to his family in the audience.

5. Wes _____ studies, so it's no surprise that he did _____ poorly on his finals.

Conjunctions

A *conjunction* is a word that connects. There are two types of conjunctions: coordinating and subordinating.

Coordinating Conjunctions

Coordinating conjunctions join two equal ideas. Look at the following sentence:

Kevin *and* Steve interviewed for the job, *but* their friend Anne got it.

In this sentence, the coordinating conjunction *and* connects the proper nouns *Kevin* and *Steve*. The coordinating conjunction *but* connects the first part of the sentence, *Kevin and Steve interviewed for the job,* to the second part, *their friend Anne got it.*

Following is a list of all the coordinating conjunctions. In this book, they are simply called *joining words.*

Coordinating Conjunctions (Joining Words)			
and	so	nor	yet
but	or	for	

For more on coordinating conjunctions, see information on joining words in "Run-Ons," pages 108–110, and "Sentence Variety I," pages 126–128.

Practice

10

Write a coordinating conjunction in each blank. Choose from the following: *and, but, so, or, nor*. Use each conjunction once.

1. Either Jerome _____ Alex scored the winning touchdown.

2. I expected roses for my birthday, _____ I received a vase of plastic tulips from the discount store.

3. The cafeteria was serving liver and onions for lunch, _____ I bought a sandwich at the corner deli.

4. Marian brought a pack of playing cards _____ a pan of brownies to the company picnic.

5. Neither my sofa _____ my armchair matches the rug in my living room.

_____ 7. The tires on my Chevy are worn, but the car itself is in good condition.

_____ 8. I could afford the monthly car payments, I did not have enough money to pay for insurance as well.

Standard English Verbs

_____ 9. Aunt Agatha sees much better when she puts on her bifocals.

_____ 10. The game was lost when the other team score a fourth-quarter touchdown.

_____ 11. At the end of the hike, we was covered with mosquito bites.

_____ 12. Martina have only three more courses to take to earn her degree.

Irregular Verbs

_____ 13. That show must be a rerun; I seen it at least twice.

_____ 14. If I had taken more notes in that class, I would have done better on the exam.

_____ 15. I accidentally throwed away the parking ticket when I cleaned out the glove compartment of my car.

_____ 16. At the end of the practice session, all the players drank Gatorade.

Subject-Verb Agreement

_____ 17. The major story on all the news programs concerns the proposed tax hike.

_____ 18. There was only two handkerchiefs left in the drawer.

_____ 19. My sister and her husband take my father bowling every Thursday night.

_____ 20. Each of my little boys need a warmer jacket for the winter.

Consistent Verb Tense

_____ 21. After I checked my bank balance, I realized I did not have enough money for a new car stereo.

_____ 22. Upon finding a seat on the bus, Ralph unfolded his newspaper, turns to the sports section, and began to read.

Pronoun Reference, Agreement, and Point of View

_____ 23. All students should try their best to get good grades.

_____ 24. My first year in college I stayed in a dorm, where they chose a roommate
for me.

_____ 25. Our company never gives bonuses to its employees, no matter how hard you
work.

Pronoun Types

_____ 26. Paula writes much better than me.

_____ 27. My sister and I have both gotten part-time jobs.

Adjectives and Adverbs

_____ 28. The children smiled so sweet that I knew they were up to something.

_____ 29. The professor spoke honestly to me about my writing strengths and problems.

_____ 30. Weighing 350 pounds, Max the Mauler was the most heaviest of the four
wrestlers in the ring.

_____ 31. Soap operas are more enjoyable to Stefan than game shows.

Misplaced Modifiers

_____ 32. At the electronics store, we bought a DVD Player that has a stop-action feature.

_____ 33. I returned the toy to the store that was broken.

Dangling Modifiers

_____ 34. While playing cards, two pizzas were eaten.

_____ 35. Glancing out the window, Felipe saw a strange car pull into the driveway.

Faulty Parallelism

_____ 36. Before I can settle down to studying, I must take out the garbage, dry the
dishes, and the leftovers have to be put away.

_____ 37. Three ways of treating a cold are bed rest, chicken soup, and taking vitamin C.

Capital Letters

_____ 38. Daylight saving time usually ends on the last sunday in October.

_____ 39. Last summer I worked as a stock boy at Target.

_____ 40. Most of the people who live in that neighborhood are doctors.

_____ 41. Vince yelled, "hurry up, the show's starting in ten minutes."

Numbers and Abbreviations

_____ 42. So far 7 students have dropped out of my math course.

_____ 43. The assignment starts on page 132 of the math book.

_____ 44. Norm's insurance co. increased his rates after he was involved in a car accident.

End Marks

_____ 45. Are you going to the church service tomorrow.

_____ 46. I wondered if I should give Terry a call.

Apostrophe

_____ 47. Lucys goal is to become the head nurse at the same hospital where her mother once worked.

_____ 48. I wasnt able to sleep at all the night after my wisdom teeth were pulled.

_____ 49. I did some careful thinking before I rejected my lawyer's advice in the matter.

_____ 50. Several storm windows' in the house are badly cracked.

Quotation Marks

_____ 51. Benjamin Franklin once wrote, "Fish and visitors begin to smell after three days."

_____ 52. I'll be with you in just a moment, the harried salesperson said."

_____ 53. If that's your opinion," said Fran, "you're more narrow-minded than I thought."

_____ 54. Time is money, the manager said, and I don't have much."

Comma

_____ 55. The dessert consisted of homemade ice cream and a choice of fresh straw-berries blueberries or peaches.

_____ 56. My brother, who lifts weights, rarely loses an argument.

_____ 57. When I opened the door to my apartment I quickly sensed that something was wrong.

_____ 58. It was supposed to rain heavily all day, but we only got a light drizzle in the morning.

Spelling

_____ 59. If I had controlled my time better this semester, I would have been a successful student.

_____ 60. Maureen has alot of definitions to study for her biology test.

_____ 61. My roommate wants to hold partys in our apartment every weekend.

_____ 62. The house we just bought has two baths and a sunken liveing room.

Omitted Words and Letters

_____ 63. As a child, I always cut the crusts my bread.

_____ 64. All three record stores in the mall have sales on select new releases.

_____ 65. All the outside doors in our house have dead-bolt lock.

Commonly Confused Words

_____ 66. I'm very sorry to hear that your not feeling well.

_____ 67. You can't judge a book by it's cover.

_____ 68. The car was going much to fast to stop at the light.

_____ 69. The tenants decided to take their landlord to court.

Effective Word Choice

_____ 70. Our car was totaled in the accident; we're lucky to be alive.

_____ 71. Without financial aid, my children are going to have a lot of trouble trying to make ends meet.